THE FOUR SEASONS

First published in the United States of America in 2025 by
Rizzoli Electa, a Division of
Rizzoli International Publications, Inc.
49 West 27th Street
New York, NY 10001
www.rizzoliusa.com

Originally published in French in 2018 as
Les saisons par les grands maîtres de l'estampe japonaise by
Éditions Hazan, an imprint of Hachette Livre, Vanves, France
www.editions-hazan.fr

For Rizzoli Electa
Publisher: Charles Miers
Associate Publisher: Margaret Rennolds Chace
Editor: Klaus Kirschbaum
Assistant Editor: Emily Ligniti
Translator: Liza Tripp

ISBN: 978-0-8478-4570-5
Library of Congress Control Number: 2024942682

Printed in China
2025 2026 2027 2028 / 10 9 8 7 6 5 4 3 2 1

Visit us online:
Instagram.com/RizzoliBooks
Facebook.com/RizzoliNewYork
X: @Rizzoli_Books
Youtube.com/user/RizzoliNY

THE FOUR SEASONS
GREAT WORKS OF JAPANESE WOODBLOCK PRINTING

Amélie Balcou

Rizzoli Electa

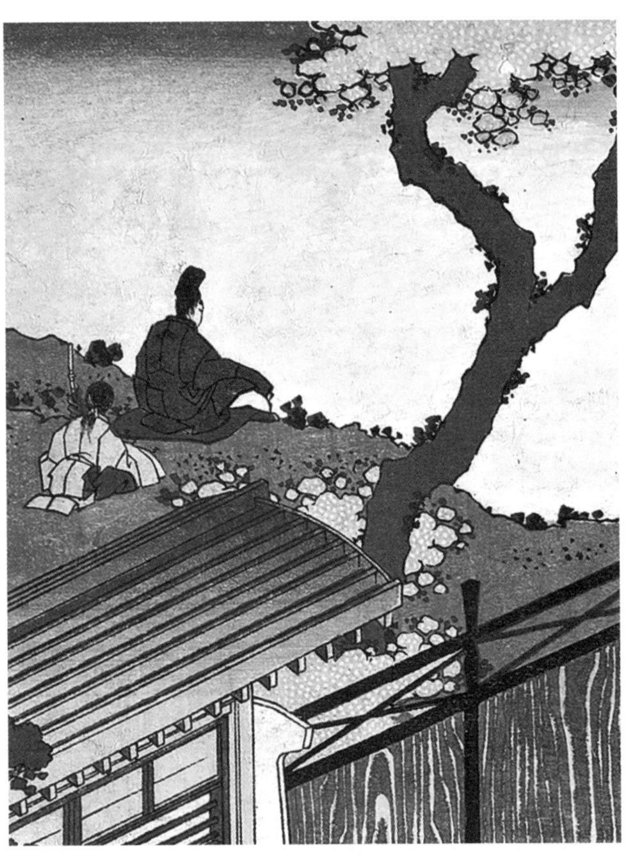

**"Surrendering fully to the contemplation
of the moon, the snow, the cherry blossoms,
and the maple leaves . . . "**

While the Japanese archipelago has seen exponential development, the people of Japan nonetheless continue to live according to nature's rhythm, with a packed calendar of seasonal celebrations and customs. The country begins the year admiring the *hatsuhinode* ("first sunrise"), then celebrates the arrival of spring with *Setsubun* in February, followed by the equinox in March, before hurrying off to the parks to view and enjoy the cherry blossoms (the custom of *hanami*). The *Hana Matsuri* flower festival celebrates Buddha's birthday in April. Nature day (*Midori no Hi*) is in May, when the rainy season (*tsuyu*) begins. Summer starts in July, along with the Star Festival (*Tanabata*), and features numerous fireworks called *hanabi* or "fire flowers." Ocean Day (*Umi no Hi*) signals the start of school vacation while Mountain Day (*Yama no Hi*) has been celebrated on August 11 since 2016. After the fall equinox, all eyes shift to the blazing leaves of the *momiji* (maple trees) and to the moon for *Tsukimi* ("moon contemplation") . . . With keen awareness of their environment (a result of Shinto and Buddhist precepts), the people of Japan keep watch all year long for the tiniest signs from nature, each a prompt for contemplation and celebration.

This intimate connection with nature has ancient roots in the literary and artistic culture of Japan, which only adopted the Gregorian calendar in 1873. The country previously followed a lunisolar calendar cycle that began in spring, around February. While the oldest accounts of the Japanese taste for nature and the seasons date back to the religious paintings of the sixth century, it was the poets that really drove the theme forward. Starting in the eighth century, poetry and imperial anthologies of *waka* (short poems) attributed great importance to the cycle of the seasons. The concept was then "codified" by the poets, who associated each month or time of the year with certain, symbolic elements of that period (weather, plants, animals, or famous places). Spring corresponded to the blooming of the cherry blossom trees, the arrival of the nightingale, fruit trees, and Mount Yoshino, which is renowned for its thousands of cherry blossoms. The cuckoo arrived with the summer sun. Fall was the season of the moon, no doubt because the days grew shorter, although the weather generally stayed mild enough to be able to go outside and contemplate it. The poets' most loved season brought to mind maple trees, the bellow of stags, the Tatsuta River, the Musashino Plain, and the Ogura and Kasuga[1] mountains. Winter coincided with the arrival of snow, the flight of wild geese, and the chirping of plovers—when the branches of *Prunus* trees, bamboo, or pines, those "three friends of winter," became covered with snow.[2]

The poets melded these seasons and months with space (landscapes and place names), forging a veritable "dream world" inhabited by nature, which would shape all the iconography and representation of the seasons for centuries to come.[3]

Painters, largely influenced by the Chinese model, adopted this iconography, which then became specific to Japan

It's winter,
and yet flower petals
fall from the sky:
beyond the clouds,
would spring come?

Kiyohara no Fukayabu
Kokin wakashū (Collection of Japanese Poems
of Ancient and Modern Times)
early tenth century

during the Heian period (794–1185) although new nature-related genres emerged, such as the paintings of the four seasons (*shiki-e*), the twelve months of the year (*tsukinami-e*), and famous places (*meisho-e*). Then, with the changes and relative stability of the Edo period (1600–1868), the theme truly flourished in the visual expression of the pictorial movement of *ukiyo-e*, which Asai Ryōi (1612?–1691) defined in the mid-seventeenth century in his *Tales of the Floating World (Ukiyo monogatari)*, published in Kyoto around 1661–1665: "Living solely in the present moment, surrendering fully to the contemplation of the moon, the snow, the cherry blossoms, and the maple leaves; singing songs, drinking wine, enjoying just by letting yourself float, float . . . like a gourd on the river, that's the floating world [*ukiyo*][4] . . . "

In calling for a world of pleasures, however ephemeral, Asai Ryōi had already placed the seasons (moon/fall, snow/winter, flower/spring), symbols of the eternal renewal of nature, at the core of the concept of *ukiyo-e*. Yet it is undoubtedly through the landscape genre, so conducive to representing nature and all of its variations, that the theme found its most mature expression, with Hokusai and Hiroshige leading the pack.

"Even if I were a ghost, I'd joyfully walk the moors in summer."[5]

Hokusai (1760–1849) reached the pinnacle of his career in the early 1830s when he released (with his publisher Nishimura Yohachi) one of the first great series, in a lavishly printed wide and large format,[6] uniquely dedicated to landscapes: *Thirty-six Views of Mount Fuji*.[7] With great mastery, he inventively combined the principles of Western perspective with the Japanese pictorial tradition, while also playing with geometric shapes. The volcano is an unwavering feature, regardless of the seasons or weather. It is a spectator of the world of men and women—at times solitary and stately, at times sketched into a far-off horizon. Hokusai plays with atmospheric effects and represents the mountain as sacred in all seasons, whether whitened by snow, darkened by thunder, or reddened by the sun, lost in a foggy or sunny horizon, amidst the clouds or in a crystalline Prussian blue sky.[8]

Nature forges ahead, eternally renewed by the cycling of the seasons, while the steadfast Mount Fuji is the great sovereign, the *meisho* par excellence. Against this eternity,

Without a care for the season
Is Fuji's peak.
What season does it imagine itself
For the falling snow
To give it the coat of a young
Stag?

Ariwara no Narihira
Shin kokinshū (New Collection of Ancient and Modern Poems)
twelfth century

Hokusai sets humans, in all of their diversity, always moving and busy with daily tasks, whether at peace with a nurturing environment or grappling with a dominating, unpredictable nature. That is the entire premise of the famous *The Great Wave off Kanagawa*, which juxtaposes the fragility of life with the force of nature and unpredictability of the elements.[9] Just as he does with the eternal, Hokusai captures the instantaneous and ephemeral as well, bridging the spiritual values of Buddhist thought—according to which human possessions are ephemeral (just like the boats carried away by *The Great Wave off Kanagawa*) with Shinto philosophy, which advocates for a vision of an all-powerful nature.[10]

Hokusai did not invent the landscape genre (which he had nonetheless already extensively explored) so much as give it a leading role. The success of the series was immediate. The landscape genre addressed the new concerns of the people and the urban, upwardly mobile Chōnin, who were the primary purchasers of the prints. With the progressive decline of the Tokugawa shogunate, which had closed Japan to foreigners as of 1841 and then gradually limited movement in the country, pressure from edicts and restrictions decreased and people could finally travel as they wished.[11] The gradual development throughout the Tokugawa period of Japan's main roads, centered around Edo (the future Tokyo), Kyoto, and Osaka,[12] also made it easier to travel for pleasure or take pilgrimages to provincial monasteries or shrines.

The people of Japan rediscovered nature and took to the roads in search of famous landscapes. They reconnected with ancestral traditions, following the precepts of Buddhism and Shintoism, and celebrated the seasons—

cherry blossoms in spring, maple leaves in fall, and the first snowfalls of winter . . .

Note that while the Tokugawa maintained a certain balance in Japan, the shogunate nonetheless did not avoid famines or revolts, or establish a stable economic order. As the demographic curve rose, the Japanese scrutinized the seasons, which were a determining factor for rice farming, in particular during the difficult period of 1833–1836. This period was marked by a significant famine caused by poor weather conditions, which then led to numerous revolts and civil unrest.

From the time that *Thirty-six Views of Mount Fuji* was published, landscapes became a major genre of the *ukiyo-e* and reinvigorated the art of Japanese woodblock printing at a time when it was starting to struggle in the face of the conservative Tokugawa regime, and when it was still restricted by the reforms of the Tenpō period (1830–1845) (limitation on the number of colors, banning of erotic scenes, representations of courtesans and actors[13] . . .).

The art of Japanese woodblock printing turned toward representing nature and daily life. Soon, Hokusai completed his series with ten new boards, *View from the Other Side of Fuji* (although the images were not limited to views from the north side of the volcano) and starting in 1834 began his black-and-white series *One Hundred Views of Mount Fuji*. During those years, he published new series of *meisho-e*, such as *Remarkable Views of Bridges* and *A Tour of Waterfalls in Various Provinces,* as well as series devoted to flowers and birds (*kachō-ga*). He adopted the originally Chinese theme of *Setsugekka* (*Snow, Moon, and Flowers*), which continued to grow in importance, combining the three most important seasons in the Japanese imagination—spring (flowers), fall (moon), and winter (snow).[14] His last series, *A True Mirror of Chinese and Japanese Poems*, along with his *One Hundred Poems Explained by the Nurse*, still serve as a foundation for representing the seasons and are in and of themselves a distillation of the heritage of the *waka* poets, as Hokusai indeed illustrated each of his panoramas with a poem.

"From the city of the East I leave, and without a brush, to see new landscapes . . . "

Following in Hokusai's footsteps, Hiroshige (1797–1858) received acclaim starting in 1833–1834 with his *Fifty-three Stations of the Tōkaidō*, which illustrated all of the legs on the "eastern sea route," the first of the "Five Roads of Edo" (or *Gokaidō*) of the Tokugawa shogunate, along with the Nakasendō (or Kiso Kaidō), the Kōshū Kaidō, the Ōshū Kaidō, and the Nikkō Kaidō. Connecting Edo, the seat of the shogun, to Kyoto, the imperial capital, the Tōkaidō stretched across some 311 miles, starting at Nihon-bashi, "the bridge of Japan," and ending at the Sanjō Ōhashi, in Kyoto.[15] In the *meisho-e* tradition, Hiroshige immortalized each of the fifty-three stations (*shukuba*) scattered along the most frequented road of Japan. The route was ideal for providing lively scenes, since at that time people were developing a taste for travel and continued to be fascinated by nature. Furthermore, the system of *sankin-kōtai* had already greatly energized the route throughout the Edo period, favoring the comings and goings of numerous samurais, who crossed the Tōkaidō accompanied by their entourages and servants. Established in 1635 to limit the risk of rebellion, this system compelled the daimyo military aristocracy to divide their time between their own land and the shogunal capital, where their families were forced to stay. While in times of peace the daimyo's authority was declining, having been weakened by this alternating residence system, the importance of the upwardly mobile urban and merchant Chōnins was simultaneously starting to grow, which boosted trade as well as the development and frequenting of interior roads.

Therefore, during the first half of the nineteenth century, the winding paths of the Tōkaidō, brimming with picturesque sites, were taken as much by travelers, merchants, and pilgrims as by samurais and daimyo. The amalgamation of all those social classes made for a great living theater, which Hiroshige discovered when he first traveled the Tōkaidō in 1832. He was fascinated by nature, the procession of daimyo, the merchants and their heavy loads, travelers climbing mountains, battling the rain or the snow or welcomed in by courtiers . . . Like Hokusai, he played with perspective and geometric shapes, juxtaposing movement and stillness, the stasis of the landscape with human restlessness. A virtuoso, he alternated flat tints of color with subtle shading, played with light or transparency, and even sometimes eliminated facial features, which gave his prints a poetic, mysterious aura. He became focused, above all, on the effects of atmosphere, climate phenomena, the cycle of the seasons, rain, storms, wind, snow, or fog, and the different times of day—dawn, dusk, or moonlight (climate is incidentally a constant concern in his travel journals, where each entry begins with an indication

> "The master Hokusai published a series of one hundred views
> before I did. In it, he transformed Mount Fuji and nature to create
> his own world. But I can only copy the nature of things.
> Therefore, my works are like photographs."
>
> Hiroshige, preface to *One Hundred Views of Mount Fuji*, 1859 (1857)
> (posthumous)

of the weather, such as "cloudy," "clear," "rain," or "snow").[16] His statement that he could only "copy the nature of things" was exceedingly modest. He did not limit himself to reproducing reality, but instead transformed it and interpreted it with a specific sensitivity, often tinged with humor. His imagination prompted him to play with the seasons, and he sometimes preferred to transpose a summer landscape to the middle of winter, under the snow or rain, as with his images of the Kanbara or Kameyama stations.

Here, too, success was immediate. Hiroshige, who had already explored the landscape genre with his *Famous Places in the Eastern Capital* (1831–1832), made use of the trend of *meisho-ki* ("guides to famous places"), which was growing at the turn of the nineteenth century. Following the huge success of *Tōkaidōchū Hizakurige* (*Shank's Mare*) by Jippensha Ikku, a comic novel recounting the adventures of two travelers, numerous guides on the routes from Japan and the Tōkaidō appeared (Asai Ryōi had already published a six-volume guide to the Tōkaidō in 1660, *Tōkaidō meisho-ki* ["Great Sites on the Eastern Sea Route"[17]]).

In addition to the Hōeidō edition of *Fifty-three Stations of the Tōkaidō*, Hiroshige devoted more than thirty series to this route, in various formats, and dreamt up numerous other topographic series. With Keisai Eisen (1790–1848), he made the *Sixty-nine Stations of the Kiso Kaidō*, which linked Edo to Kyoto, between 1834 and 1835. From 1853 to 1856 he published his *Famous Places in the Sixty-odd Provinces of Japan*, which featured seventy boards. His ambitious collection of 119 prints, *One Hundred Famous Views of Edo*, appeared from 1856 to 1859. Toward the end of his life, he took on the theme of Mount Fuji, which had been so dear to Hokusai, and made his *Thirty-six Views of Mount Fuji* and his *One Hundred Views of Mount Fuji*, both of which were published posthumously in 1859.

Hiroshige and Hokusai both had a considerable influence on the landscape genre, not only in Japan but also in the West (specifically the impressionists), and few artists proved to be as innovative and prolific in their treatment of seasons and atmosphere. Among the last Japanese landscape masters, Hasui (1883–1957) was the famous representative of the *shin-hanga* movement ("new engravings"), which updated the technique of wood engraving in the first half of the twentieth century. He was without a doubt one of the only print artists that was as committed to depicting the seasons. A tireless traveler, like Hokusai and Hiroshige before him, he painted the mountains and rivers of the countryside just as much as cities, in somber, snow-covered settings, or hot, sunny ones. With his *Twenty Views of Tokyo* and *Selected Views of the Tōkaidō*, he took his place in the line of great *ukiyo-e* artists of landscape series. Like his predecessors, he researched the effects of atmosphere and adopted the iconography of the seasons, all while asserting his own, nuanced style. Yet while the human figure was fundamental for Hokusai, and, above all, for Hiroshige, Hasui only rarely used it. He only ever populated his landscapes as an exception, depicting solitary characters, their backs often turned, as in his well-known and deeply wistful *Snow at Zōjōji Temple* prints. Along with Shinsui Itō (1898–1972), and Hiroshi Yoshida (1876–1950) in his wake, he revived the timeless theme of the seasons in printing. He did so at a time when the art form had been disrupted by the major changes of the second half of the twentieth century, thereby merging the unalterable cycle of nature with a now modern landscape.

The theme lived on and their work became inseparable in the collective imagination with that of artists like Hiramatsu Reiji (b. 1941), Kataoka Tamako (1905–2008), Togyū Okumara (1889–1990), or Atsushi Uemura (b. 1933), and can even be seen in the world of animated films. Indeed, the relationship between man and nature is essential in the work of Hayao Miyazaki (b. 1941), the director of commercially successful films like *Princess Mononoke* (1997), *Spirited Away* (2001), and *Howl's Moving Castle* (2004). All of these feature films take place in a dreamlike world where the idea of a sovereign nature reclaiming its rights is ever-present. Nature bears witness to the concerns of a country that had already experienced death by nuclear energy, at a time when humanity's imprint on the planet is now irreversible and global warming has disrupted the rhythm of the seasons.

[1] Jacqueline Pigeot, "Un imaginaire de la nature," in Christine Shimizu (ed.), *Le Japon au fil des saisons : collection Robert et Betsy Feinberg*, exhibition catalogue (Paris, Musée Cernuschi, September 19, 2014–January 11, 2015). Paris: Paris Musées, 2014, pp. 31–37.

[2] Christine Shimizu, "La nature et les saisons de la peinture japonaise," in Ibid., pp. 9–17.

[3] Claire-Akiko Brisset, "Peinture et saisons au Japon: une poétique du temps et du lieu," in Ibid., pp. 39–45.

[4] Hélène Bayou, *Images du Monde flottant. Peintures et estampes japonaises XVII-XVIII siècles*. Paris: Réunion des musées nationaux, 2004, p. 20. Donald Jenkins, "The Roots of Ukiyo-e: Its Beginnings to the Mid-eighteenth Century," in *The Hotei Encyclopedia of Japanese Woodblock Prints*. Amsterdam: Hotei Publishing, 2005, pp. 47–74.

[5] Hokusai translated by Nelly Delay, *L'Estampe japonaise*. Paris: Hazan, 2004, pp. 201–257.

[6] The set is printed in the Oban format, which corresponds to approximately 10 × 14.5–14.9 in. (25.5 × 37–38 cm).

[7] Jocelyn Bouquillard, *Hokusai: Les Trente-Six Vues du mont Fuji*. Laure Dalon, *Hokusai*, exhibition catalogue (Paris, Grand Palais, Galeries nationales, October 1, 2014–January 18, 2015). Paris: Réunion des musées nationaux, 2014, p. 282.

[8] Artificial pigment imported from the Netherlands and used in Edo as of 1829, which is deeper and more intense than the natural blues used up to that

point. It was so popular starting in the early 1830s that Nishimura Yohachi launched, simultaneously with the colored version of the *Thirty-six Views of Mount Fuji*, an edition in *aizuri-e*, consisting of boards that were essentially printed in blue.

[9] Jocelyn Bouquillard, Op. cit.

[10] Ibid.

[11] Nelly Delay, Op. cit.

[12] Jocelyn Bouquillard, Op. cit.

[13] Ibid.

Sara Elizabeth Thompson, "Censorship and Ukiyo-e Prints. Japanese Woodblock Prints," in *The Hotei Encyclopedia of Japanese Woodblock Prints*, Op. cit., pp. 318–322. Nelly Delay, Op. cit., pp. 57–59. Two other censorship incidents were particularly important: the Kyōhō reforms in the early 1720s and the Kansei reforms in the 1790s (cf. Sara Elizabeth Thompson).

[14] Christine Shimizu, "Seasons and Places in Yamato Landscape and Painting," *Ars Orientalis*, vol. 12, 1981, pp. 1–18; Christine Shimizu, "La nature et les saisons dans la peinture japonaise," Op. cit.

[15] Jocelyn Bouquillard, *Le Tōkaidō de Hiroshige*. Paris: Bibliothèque de l'image, 2002, p. 5.

[16] Nelly Delay, Op. cit.

[17] Jilly Traganou, *The Tōkaidō Road: Traveling and Representation in Edo and Meiji Japan*. New York: Routledge, 2004, pp. 103–113.

1| A crowd of passersby and Chōnin take advantage of spring's arrival to gather under the pale pink blooms of cherry blossom trees from Mount Goten to Shinagawa, the first leg of the route from Tōkaidō. They bask in an idyllic, lush, and verdant countryside dotted with small teahouses, in harmony with their environment. In the distance, behind Sagami Bay, Mount Fuji stands out against a clear sky, intensified by the use of Prussian blue.

2| For his series on the theme of *Setsugekka* (*Snow, Moon, and Flowers*), which refers to the three most important seasons (spring/flowers, fall/moon, winter/ snow), Hokusai drew a view from Mount Yoshino, a popular spot for *hanami* ("contemplation of the cherry trees") to symbolize spring. As a group of merchants climbs the steep paths of the mountain, a few residences and the *torii* ("portal") of a sanctuary slip behind a cloud of cherry blossom trees, lost to an ocean of pale pink flowers.

3| In *One Hundred Poems Explained by the Nurse*, Hokusai illustrated the *waka* poems of the *One Hundred Poems by One Hundred Poets*, the famous eighth-century anthology compiled by Fujiwara no Teika (1162–1241). Here, illustrating a poem by Ōnakatomi no Yoshinobu (921–991), imperial guards warm up by a fire while the emperor, isolated within his palace, thoughtfully contemplates the horizon seated beneath a cherry blossom tree in bloom.

4| During *hanami*, a procession of Chōnin visits Mount Asuka and admires its numerous cherry blossom trees. Distributed among the trees are signs prohibiting passersby from breaking off the branches, as evoked by the *kyōka* poem by Taihaidō Nomimasu ("The snow covers the signs that forbid breaking off the cherry blossom branches, and breaks them, too"), which Hiroshige would illustrate for his *Eight Views in the Environs of Edo*, around 1838, with a new view from Mount Asuka, this time covered in snow.

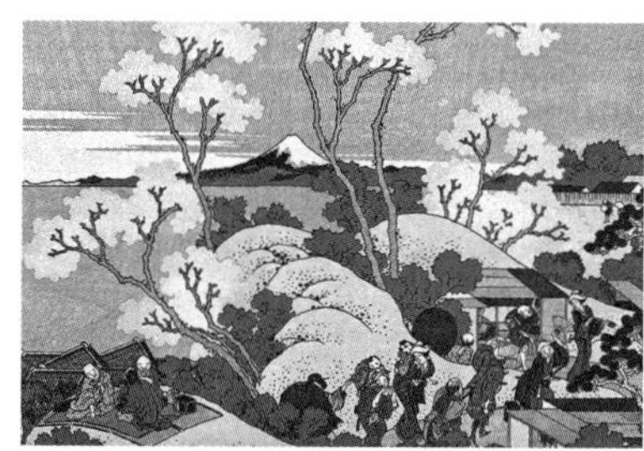

1 | Katsushika Hokusai

Fuji from Gotenyama at Shinagawa
on the Tōkaidō
Series: *Thirty-six Views of Mount Fuji*,
publisher: Nishimura Yohachi (Eijudō),
ca. 1830–1832
24.8 × 36.7 cm

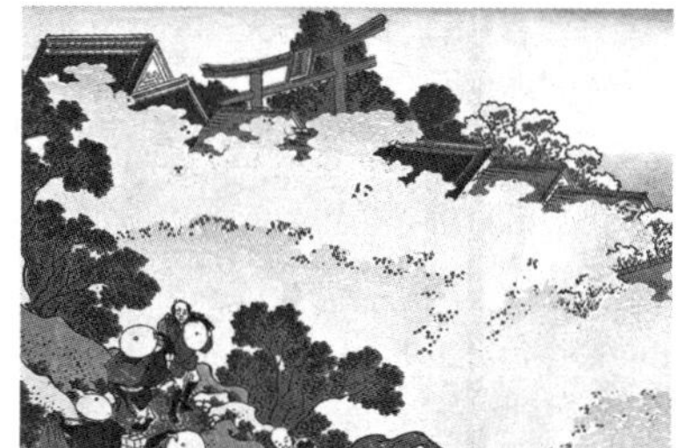

2 | Katsushika Hokusai

Cherry Blossoms at Yoshino
Series: *Setsugekka*, publisher: Nishimura
Yohachi (Eijudō), ca. 1833
25.1 × 37.1 cm

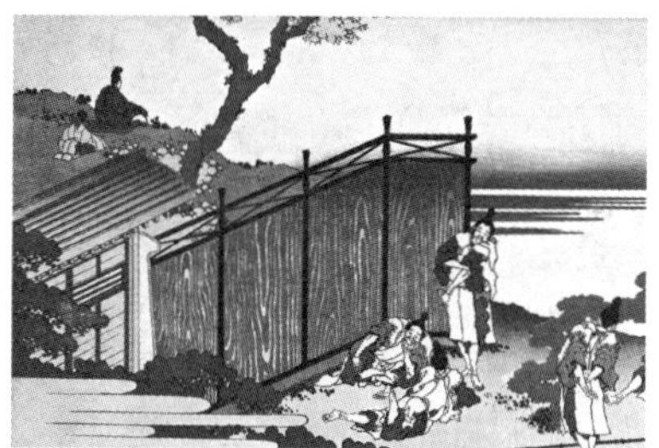

3 | Katsushika Hokusai

Poem by Ōnakatomi no Yoshinobu Ason
Series: *One Hundred Poems Explained*
by the Nurse, publisher:
Iseya Sanjirō (Eijudō), 1839
25.4 × 35.9 cm

Torches of the imperial guard; they stir up the
night, stifle the day—incessant languor.

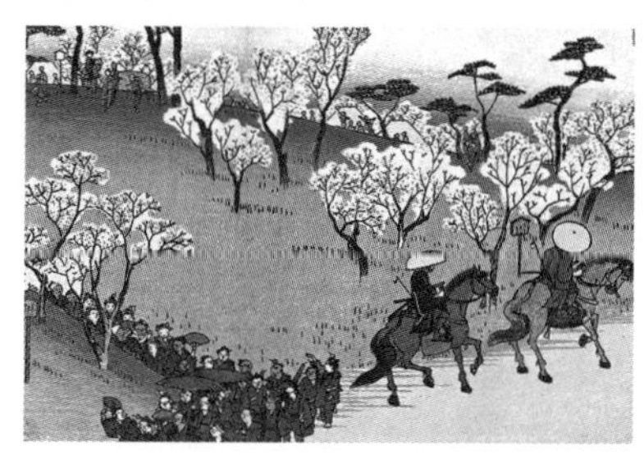

4 | Utagawa Hiroshige

Viewing Cherry Blossoms on Asuka Hill
Series: *Famous Places in Edo*, publisher:
Sanoya Kihei (Kikakudō),
ca. 1832–1834
24.1 × 36.8 cm

5| At night, a crowd of Chōnin, nobles, and courtesans are astir before the front gate of Yoshiwara, the famous red-light district of the Edo period, where samurais (idle during this peacetime period) and the middle class could surrender fully to leisure activities. Playing with one-point perspective, Hiroshige draws the view from the main street (*Nakano-chō*, "the street through the middle") which is 820 feet long and bordered by countless "green homes," restaurants, and boutiques.

6| Midono-juku was the forty-second station along the route from Kiso Kaidō, illustrated between 1835 and 1842 in an important series of woodblock prints begun by Eisen for the publisher Hōeidō, then completed by Hiroshige and the publisher Iseya Rihei. After a long and winding road from the Nojiri station, travelers reached the prosperous fields of Midono: here a man crosses the path of a woman and her child, who have come to bring refreshment to the farmers. In the background there is a tiny little path leading to the *torii* ("entry gate") to a Shinto sanctuary and its garden of plum trees.

7| For this small-format edition of *Fifty-three Stations of the Tōkaidō*, published by Sanoya Kihei, Hiroshige represents a teahouse at the Ishibe station. The viewer peels back the curtains of the establishment and discovers the life of its occupants through its *shoji* (sliding panels), which open out onto a garden where peonies and plum trees are in bloom. To the right, a noble is massaged by a blind man while maids prepare tea for him.

8| At the end of his life, Hiroshige made two beautiful series on the theme of the Six Tama Rivers. Here, in vertical format, the poet Ariwara no Narihira (825–880), an aristocrat who had been exiled for his scandalous affair with imperial concubine Fujiwara no Takaiko (836–891), takes a break alongside a shallow stream. On horseback, accompanied by his two domestics, he thoughtfully contemplates the delicate yellow flowers of a *yamabuki* bush.

5 | Utagawa Hiroshige
Night Cherry Blossoms at Yoshiwara
Series: *Famous Places in Edo*, publisher:
Sanoya Kihei (Kikakudō),
ca. 1835–1838
24.9 × 36.5 cm

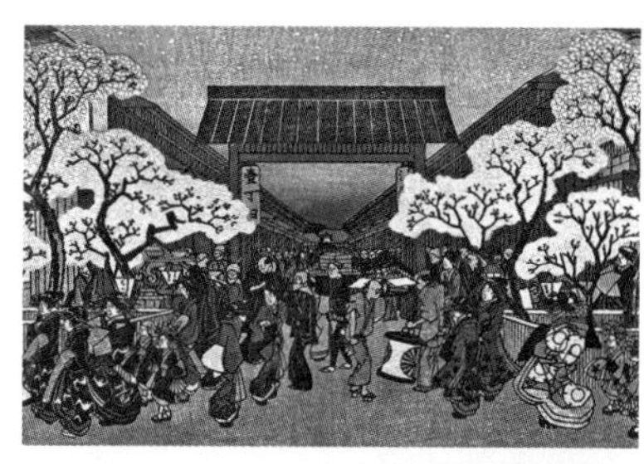

6 | Utagawa Hiroshige
Midono
Series: *Sixty-nine Stations of the Kiso Kaidō*,
publisher: Iseya Rihei (Kinjudō),
ca. 1835
25.4 × 38.1 cm

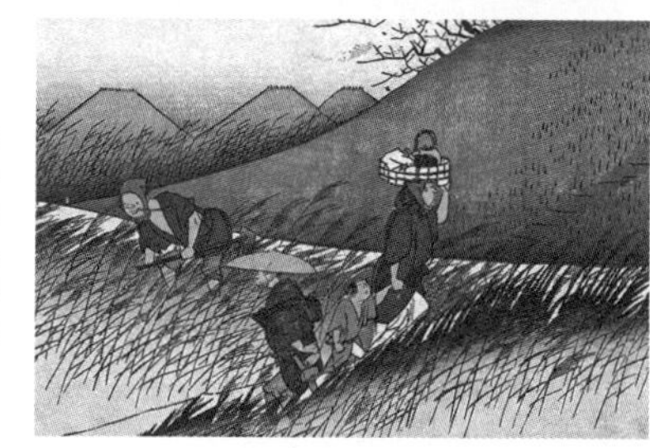

7 | Utagawa Hiroshige
Ishibe
Series: *Fifty-three Stations of the Tōkaidō*,
publisher: Sanoya Kihei (Kikakudō),
ca. 1838
16.5 × 21.9 cm

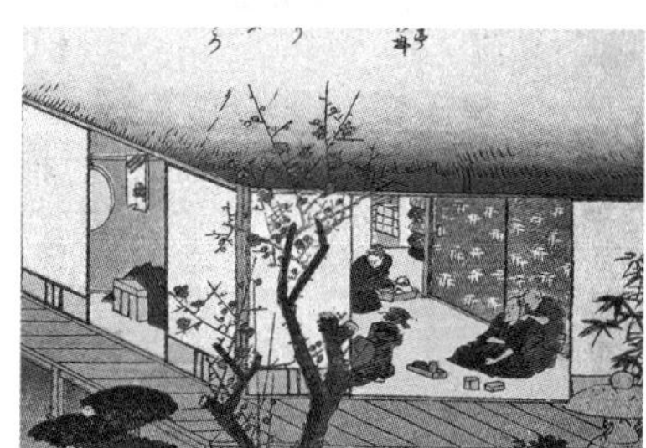

8 | Utagawa Hiroshige
The Tama River at Ide, Yamashiro Province
Series: *Six Jewel Rivers from Various
Provinces*, publisher: Maruya Kyūshiro,
November 1857
32.9 × 22.8 cm

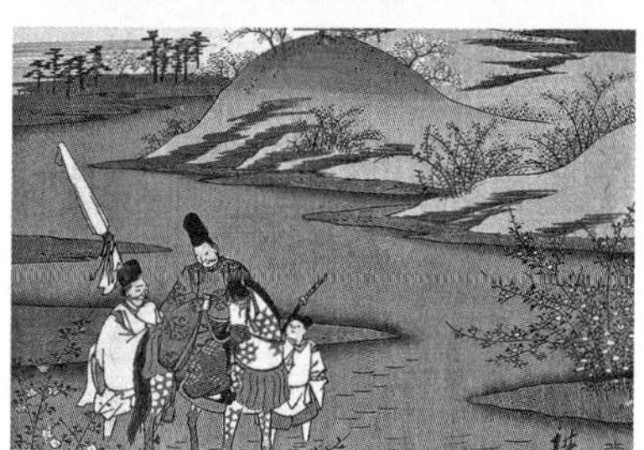

9| For the same series, illustrating a poem by Nōin (988–1058), a woman from the court (perhaps a poetess) and her servant thoughtfully observe the flight of plovers, a sign of the rainy season. Behind the two people, the Tama River winds through a steep and somber landscape, revealing a few residences. In the distance, while the setting sun casts various shades of pink, a ship continues its path between the mountains.

10| In the distance, Mount Tsukuba (Hiroshige's preferred subject) stands out against a blazing morning sky. Hiroshige uses a unique composition, offering a view from the Sumida River from the round window of a teahouse. Behind the magnolia branches, the water, dotted with little boats, winds through a luxurious, mountain landscape. On the shore, the *torii* of the Suijin shrine is barely visible.

11| An iconic woodblock print by Hiroshige, which Vincent van Gogh offered his own rendition of in 1887 (*Japonaiserie: Flowering Plum Tree*). This view of the original composition shows the garden of plum trees in the Kameido Tenjin Shrine, from the branches of a tree that might be the Garyūume ("dragon at rest"), which blew away in 1910 during a flood. The tree was famous for its thick, knotty trunk, as well as for the scent of its flowers. Behind a few passersby, the dawn is depicted in shades of pink, red, and white.

12| A source of inspiration for Claude Monet and his famed water garden in Giverny, Hiroshige depicts, behind a purple wisteria vine with flowers tumbling down in a cascade, a *taiko-bashi* ("drum-bridge," originally from China, so named because its reflection in the water supposedly gives it the shape of a drum), with an exaggerated arch. In the distance, on the opposite bank, behind a few people strolling, lies the vast garden of plum trees of the Kameido Tenjin Shrine, beneath a glowing morning sky.

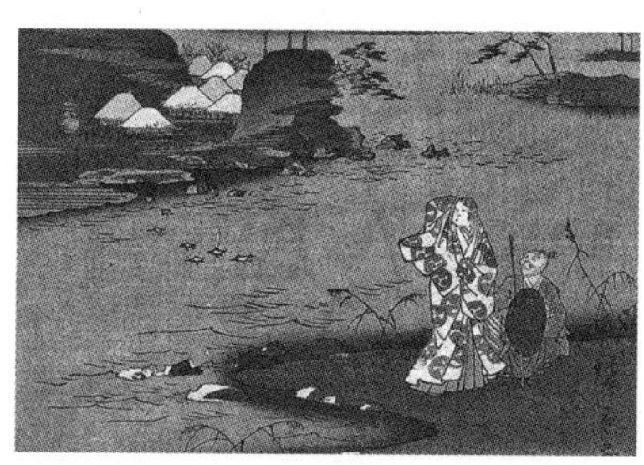

9 | Utagawa Hiroshige
The Noda Tama River in Mutsu Province
Series: *Six Jewel Rivers from Various
Provinces*, publisher: Maruya Kyūshiro,
November 1857
32.8 × 22.9 cm

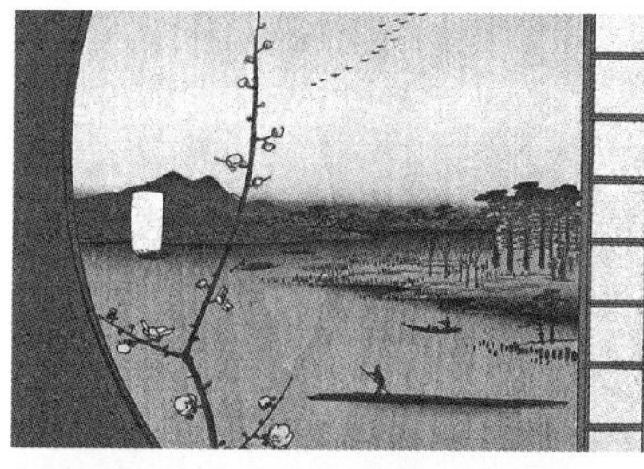

10 | Utagawa Hiroshige
*View from Massaki from the Suijin Shrine,
Uchigawa Inlet, and Sekiya*
Series: *One Hundred Famous Views of Edo*,
publisher: Uoya Eikichi (or Sakanaya
Eikichi), August 1857
33.3 × 22.1 cm

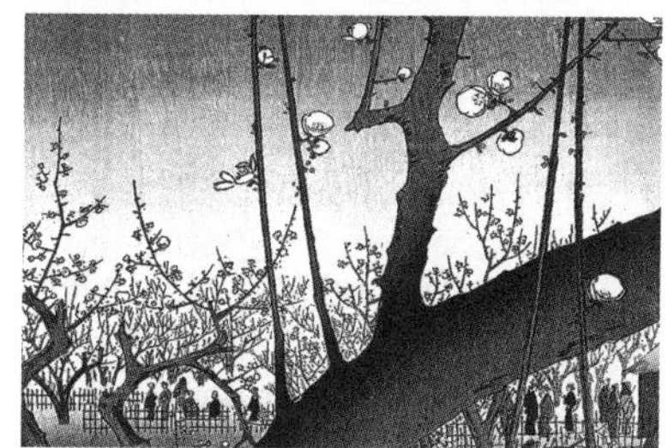

11 | Utagawa Hiroshige
The Plum Garden at Kameido
Series: *One Hundred Famous Views of Edo*,
publisher: Uoya Eikichi (or Sakanaya
Eikichi), November 1857
32.5 × 21.9 cm

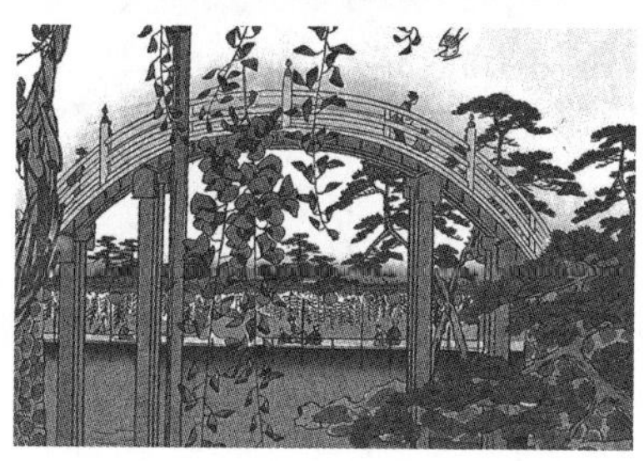

12 | Utagawa Hiroshige
In the Kameido Tenjin Shrine Compound
Series: *One Hundred Famous Views of Edo*,
publisher: Uoya Eikichi (or Sakanaya
Eikichi), July 1856
36.2 × 24.8 cm

13| The theme of rain was explored extensively by Hiroshige and the *ukiyo-e* artists, notably to illustrate the rainy season that concluded spring. Here, surprised by a downpour, a group of passersby on the Shin-Ōhashi ("new big bridge") protect themselves from the rain. In the background, behind a raft, the sky darkened by the storm provides the tiniest glimpse of the port zone of Atake, on the opposite riverbank. The view inspired Vincent van Gogh so much that he made a copy of it in 1887 (*Japonaiserie: Bridge in the Rain*).

14| For this Tōkaidō edition published by Ezakiya Tatsuzō, Hiroshige represents, for the Tsuchiyama station, travelers crossing the neck of the Suzuka in the rain, as the place was known to be prone to significant precipitation, in particular during the rainy season. Arriving before it, a procession of daimyo struggles to continue their path through the steep region. All bundled up, two porters clear the way, their feet covered in mud and their backs hunched with effort.

15| While he was one of the most popular painters of the nineteenth century, the prolific Kunisada nevertheless did very few landscapes. Here, for this bucolic scene full of travelers and peasants, he made exceptional use of the color blue to depict the rain. In the foreground, alongside a fisherman bundled up in red clothing, a stableman washes his horse in the water of a pond.

16| For his *Famous Places in Edo*, Hiroshige draws the little Shinto shrine on Mount Atago, perched 85 feet high, south of the Edo palace, recognizable by its large stone staircase. Dominating over all of Edo, its position made it a privileged watchpoint for preventing fires (the main *kami* venerated at the temple was the god of fire, Homusubi no Mikoto). Just after the rain, pilgrims take advantage of a sunny spell to rest. Looking for an atmospheric effect, Hiroshige uses the rare motif of a rainbow.

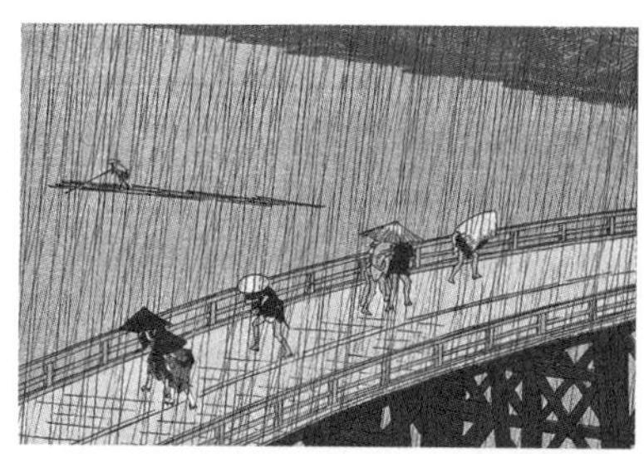

13 | Utagawa Hiroshige
Sudden Shower over
Shin-Ōhashi Bridge and Atake
Series: *One Hundred Famous Views of Edo*,
publisher: Uoya Eikichi (or Sakanaya
Eikichi), September 1857
34 × 24.1 cm

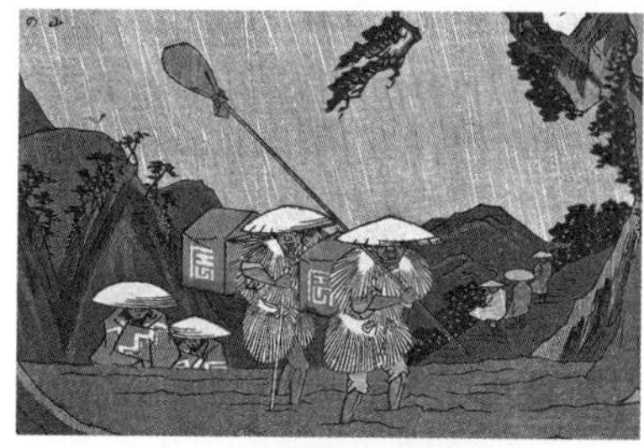

14 | Utagawa Hiroshige
Tsuchiyama, Suzuka Mountains in the Rain
Series: *Fifty-three Stations of the Tōkaidō*,
publisher: Ezakiya Tatsuzō, 1841–1844
19.4 × 31.7 cm

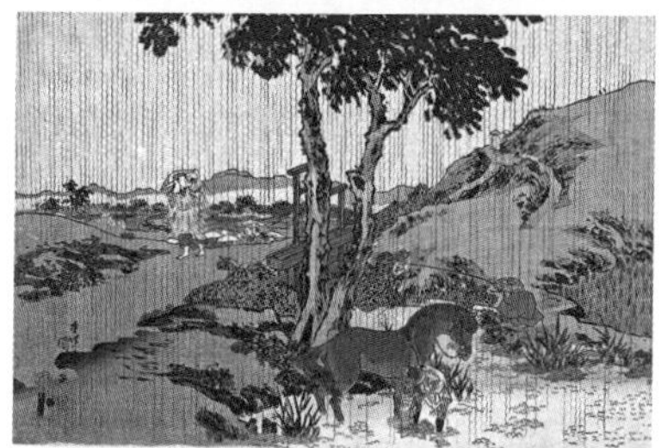

15 | Utagawa Kunisada
Rain of the Fifth Month
Publisher: Yamaguchiya Tōbei
(Kinkōdō), ca. 1832
23.8 × 36.5 cm

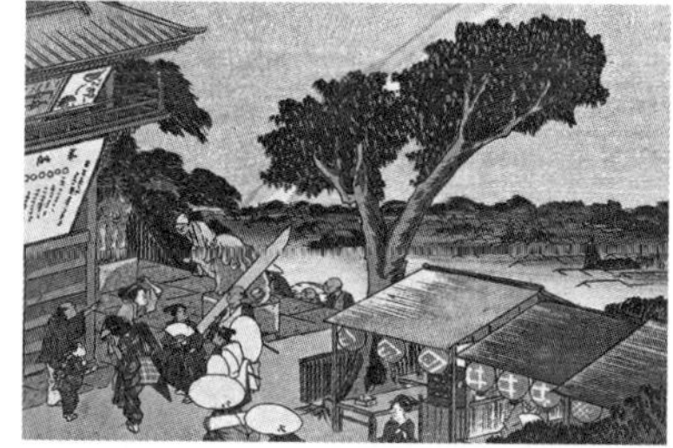

16 | Utagawa Hiroshige
On Top of Mount Atago in Shiba
Series: *Famous Places in Edo*, publisher:
Sanoya Kihei (Kikakudō),
ca. 1833–1834
24.9 × 37.3 cm

17| In the distance, surrounded by lush, green vegetation interspersed with small houses, Mount Fuji peaks out from a blanket of fog. Hokusai plays with the composition and draws a view of the volcano from the commercial Suruga street. In the foreground, signs specify the stores' specialty, the price of the merchandise, and the payment terms ("cash"). To the right, poised in unstable balance, men repair the slate on the roof of the large Mitsui textile store and battle the wind, as suggested by the two kites, which are symbols of renewal. One of them has the lucky character *ju* inscribed on it.

18| All along the road leading to the Fukuroi station, kites fly through the sky. In the upper left corner, the first, square one, decorated with a sacred lion dancing among red peonies, evokes an ancient Buddhist tale from the twelfth century recounted in the *Konjaku monogatari shū* (Japanese Tales from Times Past). A popular subject, notably in the Noh theater and later in *kabuki*, the theme referred to the pilgrimage of the priest Jakushō, who was welcomed upon his arrival to Mount Wutai in China by a lion dancing among blooms of peonies.

19| The mythical Mount Fuji is the only actor here, appearing head-on and dominating the scene per a purely Japanese style of composition excluding perspective. Exceptionally, Hokusai eliminates all human presence and centers his view around the sacred mountain. The imposing volcano, crimson beneath the sun, contrasts with the intense blue sky, which is thick with stylized white clouds.

20| Close to a fisherman, a small boat loaded with merchandise makes its way under the Mannen-bashi ("bridge of ten thousand years") that spans the Fuka, a small tributary of the Sumida River. Hokusai emphasizes the curve of the *taiko-bashi* ("drum-bridge"), which is crowded with passersby, and plays with perspective, as he often did. In the distance, near a firemen's tower, Mount Fuji dominates the banks of the Sumida, lined by homes and stores.

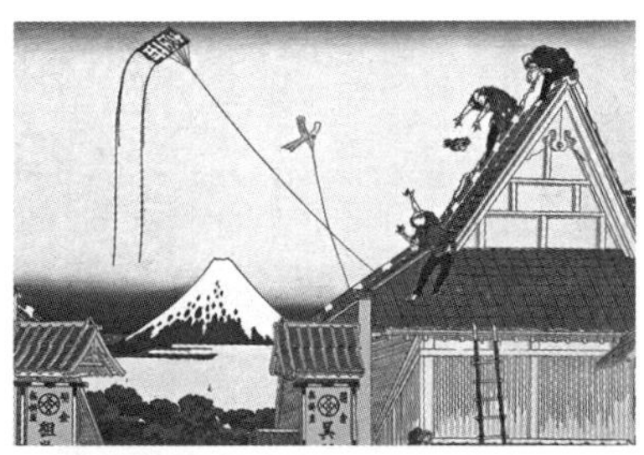

17 | Katsushika Hokusai
Mitsui Shop at Surugachō in Edo
Series: *Thirty-six Views of Mount Fuji*,
publisher: Nishimura Yohachi,
ca. 1830–1832
26 × 38.4 cm

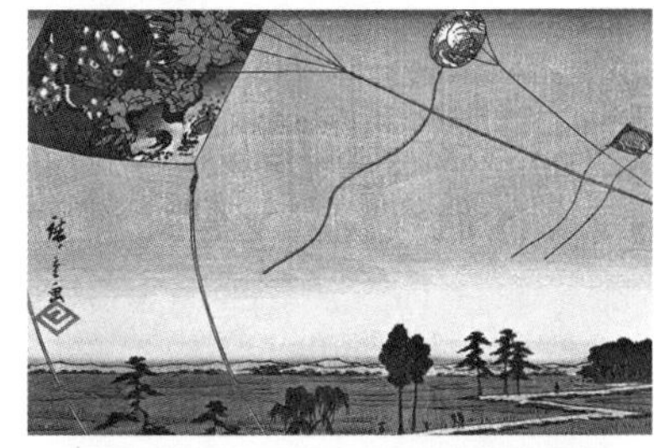

18 | Utagawa Hiroshige
Kites at Fukuroi in Tōtōmi Province,
with Akiba in the Distance
Series: *Fifty-three Stations of the Tōkaidō*,
publisher: Maruya Seijirō (Marusei,
Jukakudō), ca. 1847–1852
22.2 × 34.9 cm

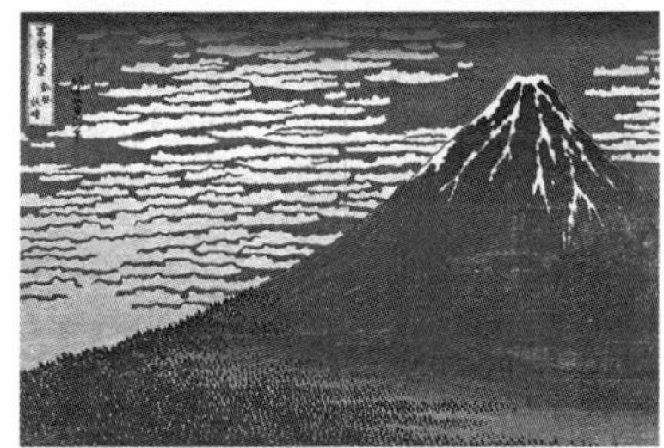

19 | Katsushika Hokusai
South Wind, Clear Sky
(also known as "Red Fuji")
Series: *Thirty-six Views of Mount Fuji*,
publisher: Nishimura Yohachi,
ca. 1830–1832
25.4 × 37.8 cm

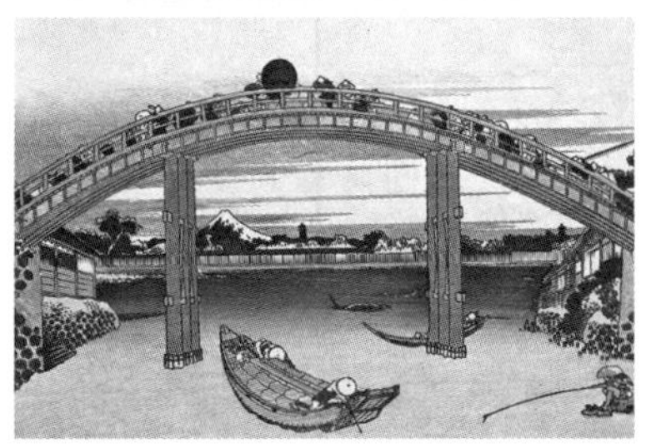

20 | Katsushika Hokusai
Under the Mannen Bridge at Fukagawa
Series: *Thirty-six Views of Mount Fuji*,
publisher: Nishimura Yohachi,
ca. 1830–1832
25.7 × 38.6 cm

21| From the terrace of the Sazai Hall at the Temple of the Five Hundred Arhats, pilgrims take advantage of a sunny day to observe Mount Fuji and its snow-covered summit. While two porters set down their loads, exhausted, a child enthusiastically points out the volcano to the other pilgrims. To his right, the wood posts of a construction site peek through the verdant vegetation, along with a few homes.

22| Summer is also the season when the weather is sufficiently mild for shell-fish gathering. Here, on the beach of the little village of Noboto, bordering the eastern coast of Edo Bay, gatherers joyfully fill up their baskets with clams under the *torii* of a Shinto shrine dedicated to a marine divinity. In the distance, Mount Fuji stands tall, watching over this happy scene where humans appear in perfect harmony with nature.

23| The Kanaya station, built along the right bank of the Ōigawa opposite Shimada, was the twenty-fourth station of the Tōkaidō. Here, crossing the river (known for its many spates), naked porters transport passersby, palanquins, or goods. To the left, a cargo of clothing is covered by a piece of fabric with the character *kotobuki* ("happiness") on it. In all likelihood it belongs to a young woman who has been promised to a Shimida man.

24| Hokusai illustrates with an abalone (*awabi*) fishing scene the poem that Ono no Takamura (802–852) composed when he returned from exile, leaving the province of Oki. While in the background, the Takamura ship sails toward Kyoto, seat of the emperor, *amas* ("sea women") dive in to collect the abalone. To the right, three women, naked up to their waists, catch their breath on a craggy rock.

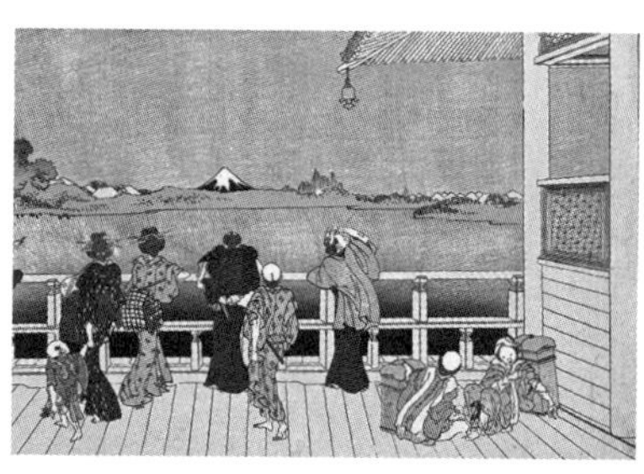

21 | Katsushika Hokusai
*Sazai Hall at the Temple
of the Five Hundred Arhats*
Series: *Thirty-six Views of Mount Fuji*,
publisher: Nishimura Yohachi,
ca. 1830–1832
25.6 × 37.1 cm

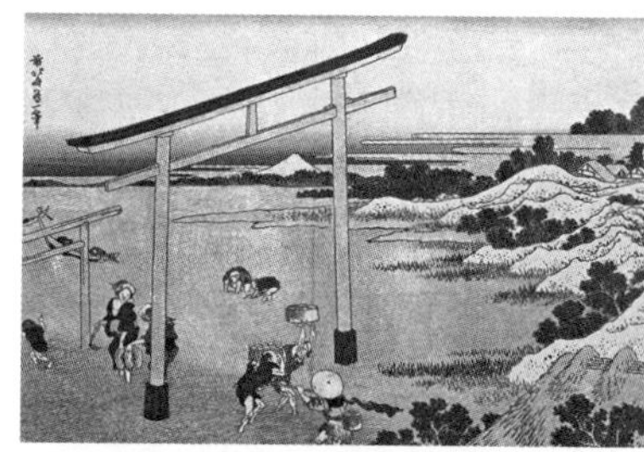

22 | Katsushika Hokusai
Noboto Bay
Series: *Thirty-six Views of Mount Fuji*,
publisher: Nishimura Yohachi,
ca. 1830–1832
26 × 38.6 cm

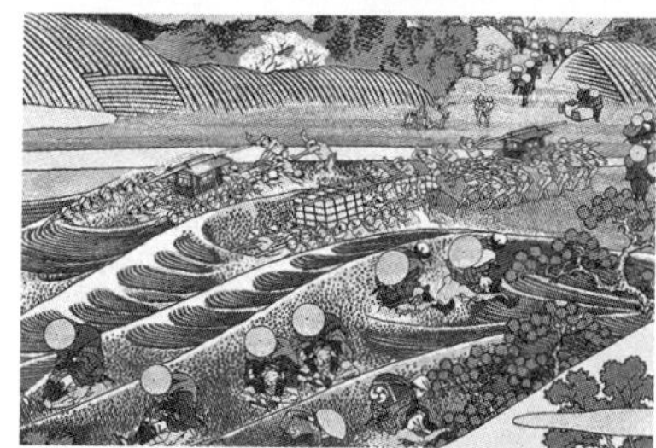

23 | Katsushika Hokusai
Fuji Seen from Kanaya on the Tōkaidō
Series: *Thirty-six Views of Mount Fuji*,
publisher: Nishimura Yohachi,
ca. 1830–1832
26 × 38.7 cm

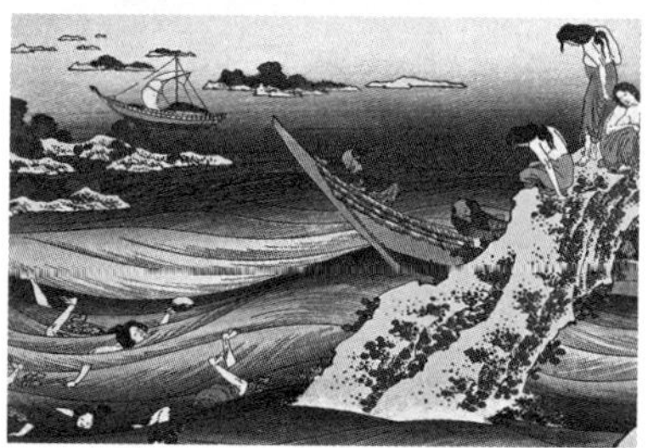

24 | Katsushika Hokusai
Poem by Sangi no Takamura (Ono no Takamura)
Series: *One Hundred Poems Explained by the
Nurse*, publisher: Iseya Sanjirō (Eijudō),
1835–1836
26.5 × 37.8 cm
*May all be warned that I will row
beyond the archipelago, to the most faraway islands,
toward the expanse of the sea, in my fishing boat!*

25| For this lesser known, and rarely reprinted, series on the famous restaurants of Edo, made between 1835 and 1842 for publisher Fujiokaya Hikotarō, Hiroshige offers a view of the Daishichi restaurant from the vast flower garden of Mukōjima, dotted with large stone lanterns. While passersby take advantage of the warm day to go for a stroll, two men try and attract the attention of the young women in the foreground, although they are met with disdain and indifference.

26| As in his *View from Massaki*, Hiroshige opts for an original composition and represents the Fukagawa River from a window of the Mannen-bashi ("bridge of 10,000 years"). In the foreground, above a barrel, a tortoise for sale seems to be watching the horizon. Beyond the river, which is littered with patches of reeds and small boats, Mount Fuji appears as the ultimate symbol of longevity (the tortoise and the bridge offer the same symbolism).

27| For his *One Hundred Famous Views of Edo*, Hiroshige depicts the oldest stable in Edo, Hatsune no baba, from a dyeing factory in the surrounding neighborhood of Kon'ya. In the middle of the stable is a wood-fire lookout tower, a familial element for the great master, who inherited the status of fire captain in 1809 from his father and, in turn, transmitted the title to his son in 1832 to fully devote himself to his art.

28| The large sheets from the dyeing factories of the Kanda neighborhood, known for the quality of their fabrics, are drying in the sun. On the left, the fabrics embellished with checkered or circular patterns are earmarked for *yukata* (summer kimonos), while the long strips in the center will be cut and used as sashes. The "fish" (*sakana*) sign on the white strips in the foreground could be a reference to the family of the publisher, Sakanaya Eikichi. As for the other white strips, they have the Hiroshige monogram on them.

25 | Utagawa Hiroshige
Mukōjima: The Daishichi Restaurant
Series: *Famous Restaurants of Edo*,
publisher: Fujiokaya Hikotarō
(Shōgendō), ca. 1835–1842
23.7 × 36 cm

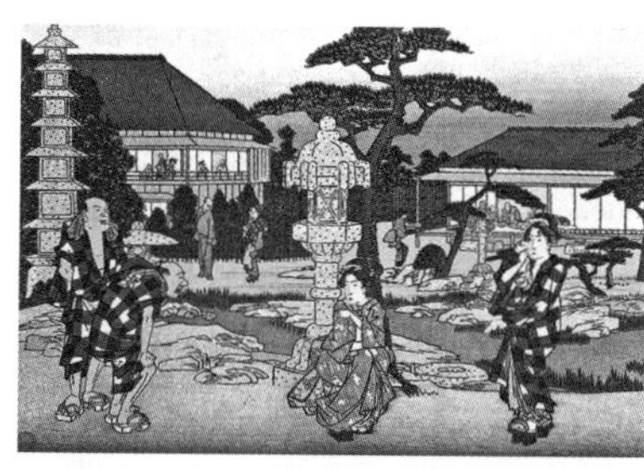

26 | Utagawa Hiroshige
Mannen Bridge, Fukagawa
Series: *One Hundred Famous Views of Edo*,
publisher: Uoya Eikichi (or Sakanaya
Eikichi), November 1857
35.7 × 24 cm

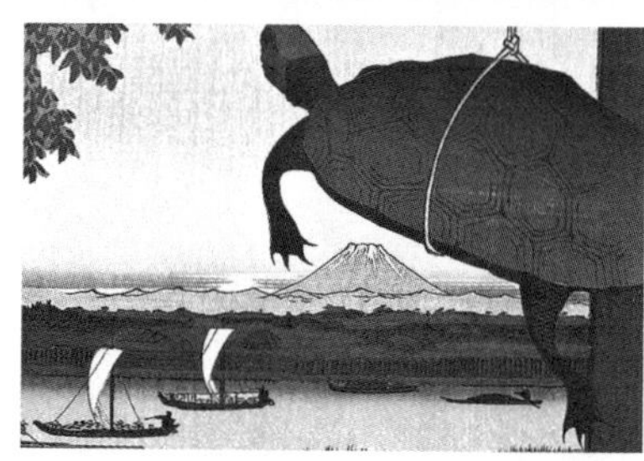

27 | Utagawa Hiroshige
The Hatsune Riding Grounds at Bakuro-chō
Series: *One Hundred Famous Views of Edo*,
publisher: Uoya Eikichi (or Sakanaya
Eikichi), September 1857
35.7 × 23.5 cm

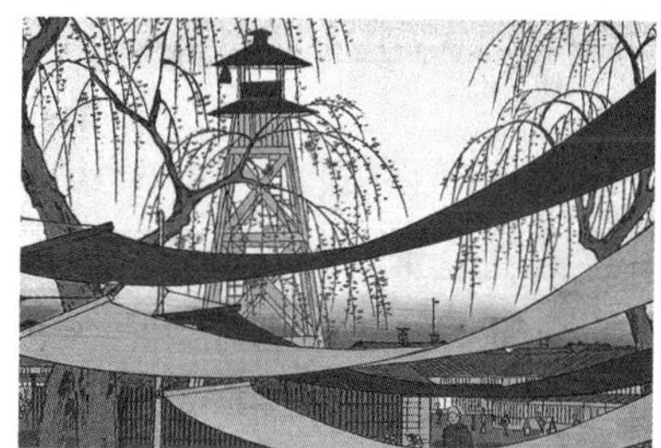

28 | Utagawa Hiroshige
Dye House at Konya-cho, Kanda
Series: *One Hundred Famous Views of Edo*,
publisher: Uoya Eikichi (or Sakanaya
Eikichi), November 1857
33 × 21.6 cm

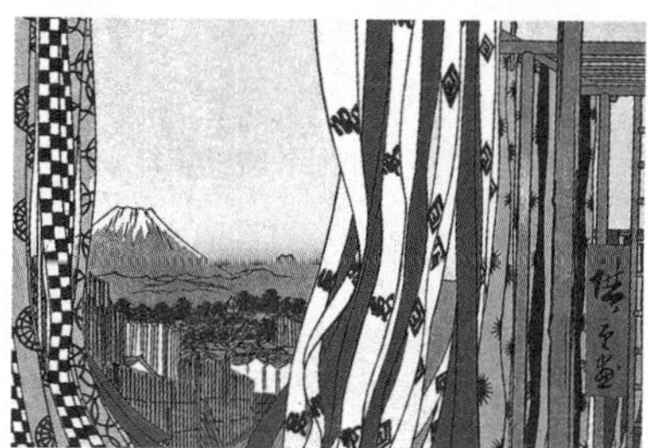

29| The famous ancestral trees on the ragged beach of Maiko, with their wide, knotty trunks, extend toward a crystal-clear sky, depicted in Prussian blue. Hiroshige uses this largely romanticized view to play with the different dimensions—lost among these great giants, the people walking and the teahouse in the background seem truly miniscule. One of them, alongside the water, points to small sails, barely visible on the horizon. Nature, grand and majestic, once again dominates over humans.

30| An extract from the famous series on the Tōkaidō from the publishing company Hoeidō, this view of the lively village of Kanagawa is inspired by the famous comic novel Jippensha Ikku (1765–1831), *Shank's Mare*, which describes the farcical adventures of two travelers. As commercial ships and fishing boats sail back and forth on the bay, the travelers cross the main street, which is edged with teahouses, inns, and lavish boutiques, trying to avoid the bawdy maids from the inns attempting to lure them inside.

31| Beneath a red summer sky, large ships cross Suruga Bay and sail alongside the cliff at Kokufu. In the foreground, five men dressed in lightweight clothes stand atop a steep, rocky bluff, coming dangerously close to the edge to watch the immense sailboats with their exaggerated proportions. As was his custom, Hiroshige played with proportions to animate the composition. On the right, a small fishing village further accentuates the seemingly enormous ships.

32| Summer is at its peak: under the rays of the sun, depicted by long, glowing bands, ships return to the steep banks of Naniwa (what is now Osaka). The high skiffs, with all sails lifted and guided by two black and white cranes, symbols of luck and longevity, head toward the port of Mount Tenpō, the landmark for sailors going back up the Aji estuary to reach the city.

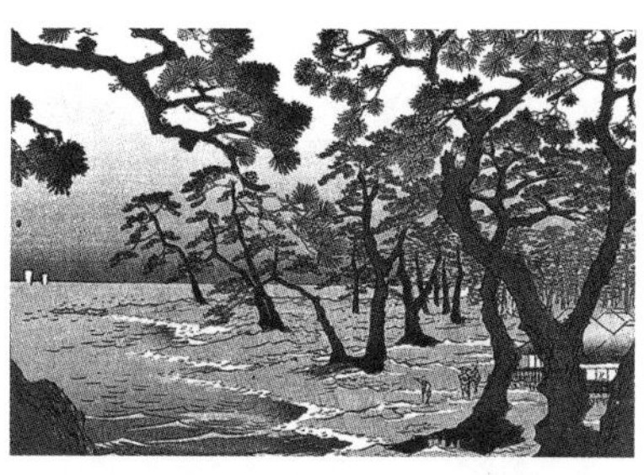

29 | Utagawa Hiroshige
Maiko Beach, Harima Province
Series: *Famous Places in the Sixty-odd Provinces of Japan*, publisher:
Koshimuraya Heisuke (Koshihei), 1853
36.2 × 24.5 cm

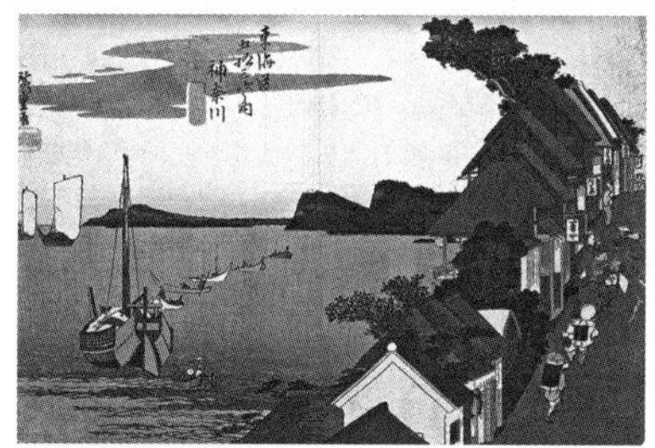

30 | Utagawa Hiroshige
Kanagawa
Series: *Fifty-three Stations of the Tōkaidō*,
publisher: Takenouchi Magohachi
(Hoeidō), ca. 1833–1834
25.8 × 35.6 cm

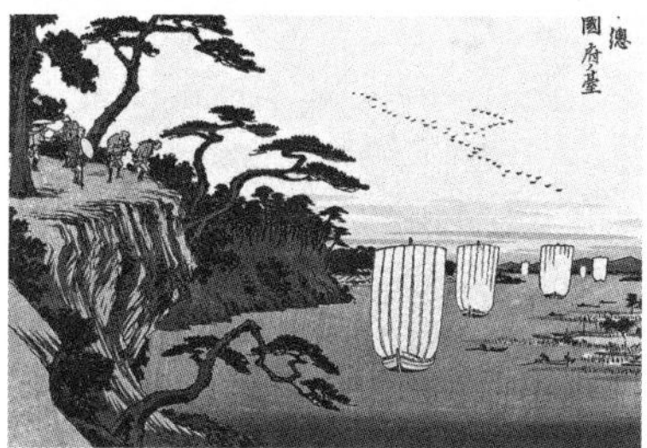

31 | Utagawa Hiroshige
The Cliff at Kokufu in Shimosa Province
Series: *Famous Views of the Kantō Region*,
publisher: Jōshūya Kinzō,
ca. 1840–1842
22.7 × 33.9 cm

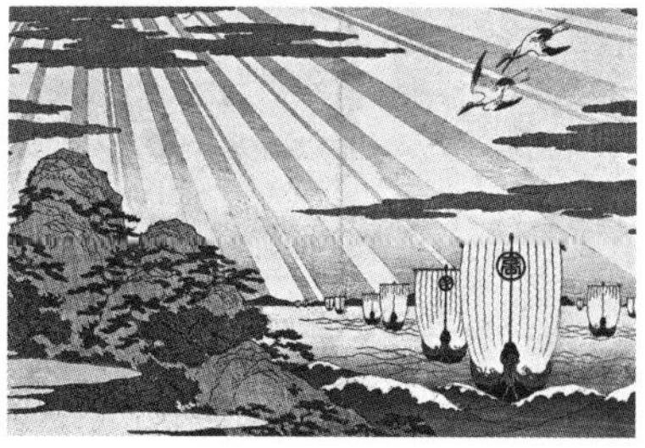

32 | Yashima Gakutei
Ships Entering Tenpozan Harbor
Series: *Famous Places in Osaka, Fine Views
of Mount Tenpo*, publisher: Shioya Kisuke
(Kōbundō), 1838
25.6 × 37.9 cm

33| The *One Hundred Poems Explained by the Nurse* are well-suited for exalting fall, since it is, by definition, the season of poets. Illustrating a poem by Kan Ke (845–903), Hokusai depicts the imperial chariot stopping in front of a temple (marked by the stone lanterns). Shaped like a shrine and covered with a maple leaf pattern, an important symbol of fall, the three-wheeled carriage is drawn by a richly harnessed steer. While the pilgrims respectfully kneel down, two courtesans whisper into the retired sovereign's ear.

34| To illustrate a poem by Sarumaru no Dayū (or Sarumaru no Taifu) from the Heian period (794–1185), Hokusai draws a procession of women returning home at sunset after a day out picking herbs and mushrooms, their bodies weighed down with baskets and rakes. In the distance, looming over this craggy landscape, turned red by the maple leaves, are two silhouettes of fawns—a subtle allusion to the poem, in stark contrast with the pink sky of the background.

35| The bridge at the Tatsuta River was a walking spot that was particularly popular in fall. To the left, a farmer lugging a basket filled with stalks of wheat struggles to climb the *taiko-bashi*, as a couple leans over to watch the efforts of the fishermen trawling in the foreground. Dusk, with all of its shades of red and ochre, contributes to the poetic feel of the scene.

36| This woodblock print illustrates a poem by the emperor Sanjō (976–1017), written while he was sick in winter 1015, and is without a doubt one of Hokusai's most solemn scenes. During a night with a full moon, members of the court honor the memory of the deceased emperor while kneeled down in front of a priest brandishing a *gohei* (a wooden purification wand to which are attached two *shide,* strips of folded paper used in Shinto rituals). On the left, a courtesan religiously holds a *tanzaku* (vertical card), wrapped in a piece of red cloth, on which the emperor's poem is probably inscribed.

33 | Katsushika Hokusai

Sugawara no Michizane (Kan Ke)
Series: *One Hundred Poems Explained
by the Nurse*, publisher: Iseya Sanjirō
(Eijudō), ca. 1839
25.4 × 37.1 cm

*This time I've come with empty hands
to the mountain of offerings
This carpet of colorful leaves and this cloth of
branches will return to the gods.*

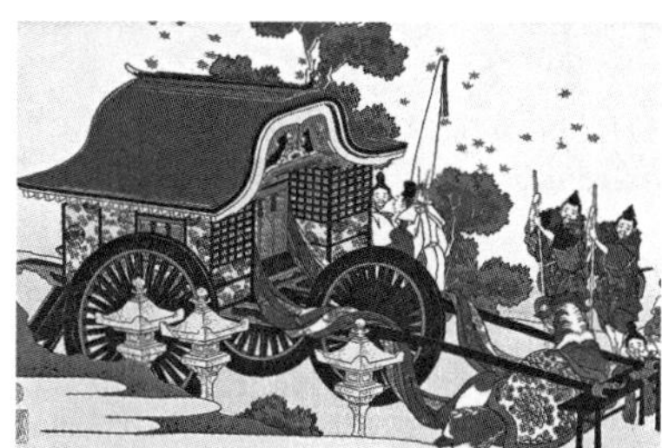

34 | Katsushika Hokusai

Sarumaru no Dayū
Series: *One Hundred Poems Explained
by the Nurse*, publisher:
Iseya Sanjirō (Eijudō), ca. 1839
25.4 × 36.5 cm

*When at the bottom of the mountain the dead
leaves underneath my steps scatter
And you hear the stag's call,
fall is sad.*

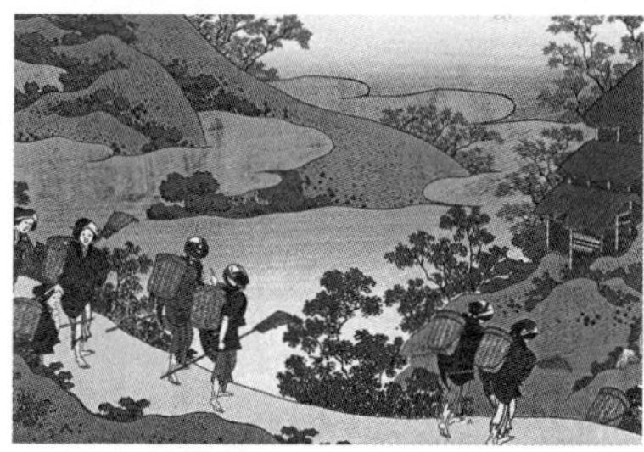

35 | Katsushika Hokusai

Ariwara no Narihira
Series: *One Hundred Poems Explained
by the Nurse*, publisher:
Iseya Sanjirō (Eijudō), ca. 1839
25.7 × 38.1 cm

*Even under the empire of the gods, no one
ever heard of a Tatsuta River
Purple too under the leaves,
the water follows its path!*

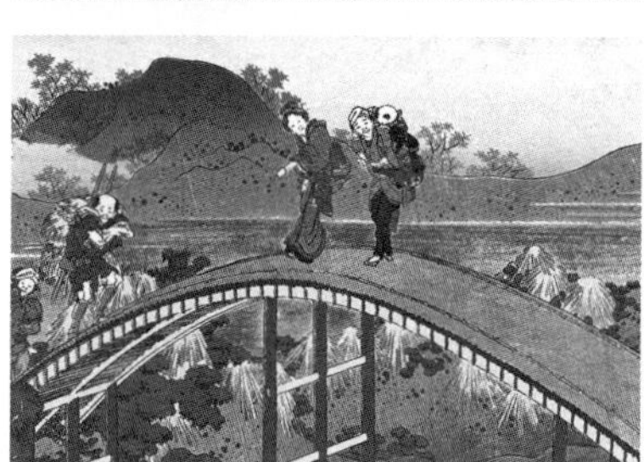

36 | Katsushika Hokusai

Sanjō-in
Series: *One Hundred Poems Explained
by the Nurse*, publisher:
Iseya Sanjirō (Eijudō), ca. 1839
26 × 37.5 cm

*Should I reluctantly prolong my days
in the floating world
For the nostalgia of a moon that leaves the night
midway in the darkness?*

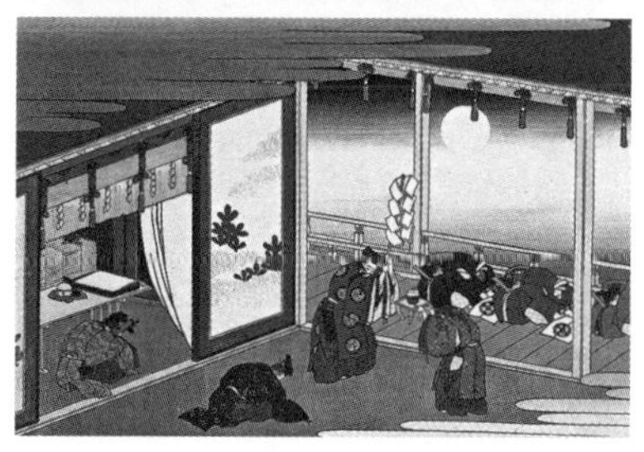

37| The noble Abe no Nakamaro (710–790) thoughtfully observes the moon's reflection in the water. The soldiers of the Chinese emperor, armed with spears and banners, kneel down and wait for him to finish his poem before arresting him (never mind that he had come to study the Chinese calendar). Associated with this autumnal view, Nakamaro is depicted as the ultimate poet, whose art predominates to the point of delaying his arrest and calling the emperor's authority into question.

38| To illustrate a poem by Fun'ya no Asayasu, Hokusai draws five young men collecting lotus nuts, a very popular food among the Japanese. Aboard a large red boat, fighting the wind and armed with long batons, they could topple into the water at any moment. Hokusai plays with the proportions to reinforce the obvious fragility of his characters. The pond, scattered with large lotus leaves, resembles a gigantic aquatic trap ready to swallow them up.

39| Between 1853 and 1856, Hiroshige made an important series of sixty-nine prints, each presenting a famous view from one of the provinces of Japan. Here, in the one from Kai, passersby risk crossing a monkey bridge steeply suspended across three fat maple trees growing on the side of the cliff. A whirlpool stirs up the river, further driving home the feeling of insecurity in the scene.

40| Celebrating the meeting of the weaver goddess Orihime and herdsman Hikoboshi, the Star Festival (*Tanabata*) marked the start of fall until 1872, per the lunisolar calendar used at that time. During the festivities in Edo, high bamboo batons were put up and decorated with a multitude of small hanging objects, streamers, and *tanzaku,* on which the Japanese wrote resolutions. In the distance, Mount Fuji emerges from beneath a coating of fog, signaling the arrival of fall.

37 | Katsushika Hokusai

Abe no Nakamaro
Series: *One Hundred Poems Explained
by the Nurse*, publisher: Iseya Sanjirō
(Eijudō), ca. 1833–1837
25.4 × 37.4 cm

*My eyes gaze across
the celestial fields: is it the moon
pointing to the Mikasa Mountains
in Kasuga?*

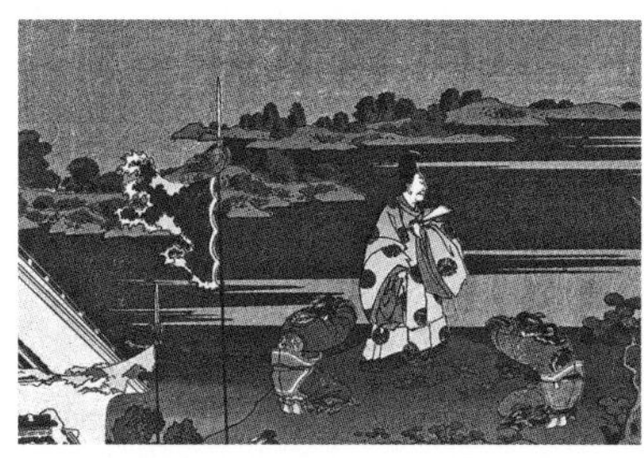

38 | Katsushika Hokusai

Fun'ya no Asayasu
Series: *One Hundred Poems Explained
by the Nurse*, publisher: Iseya Sanjirō
(Eijudō), ca. 1839
24.8 × 36.5 cm

*The kiss of fall blows
on the dew of the plain
And scatters pearls
no net can contain.*

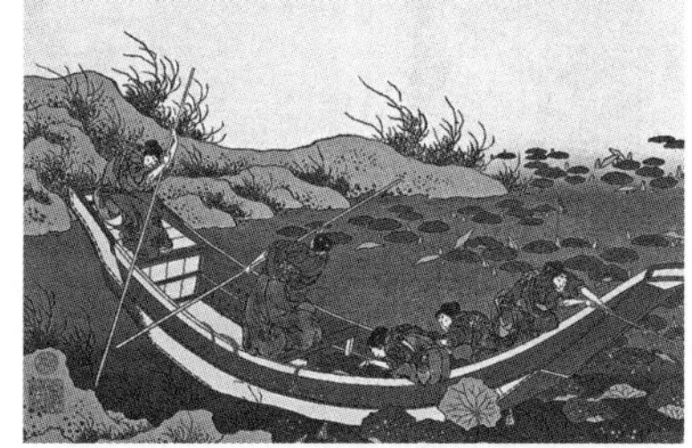

39 | Utagawa Hiroshige

The Monkey Bridge in Kai Province
Series: *Famous Places in the
Sixty-odd Provinces of Japan*, publisher:
Koshimuraya Heisuke (Koshihei),
August 1853
34 × 22.6 cm

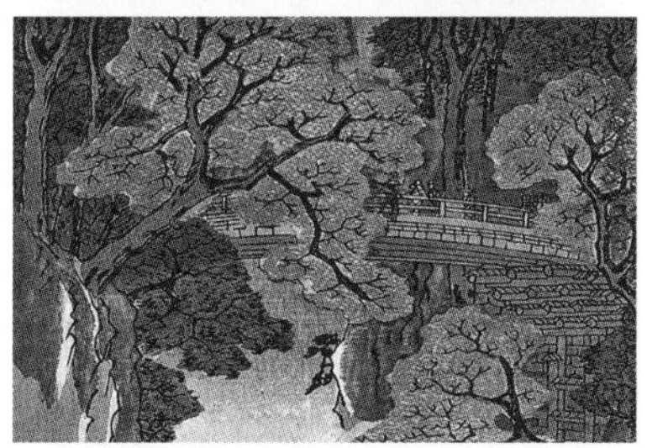

40 | Utagawa Hiroshige

Tanabata
Series: *One Hundred Famous Views of Edo*,
publisher: Uoya Eikichi
(or Sakanaya Eikichi), July 1857
35.6 × 24.4 cm

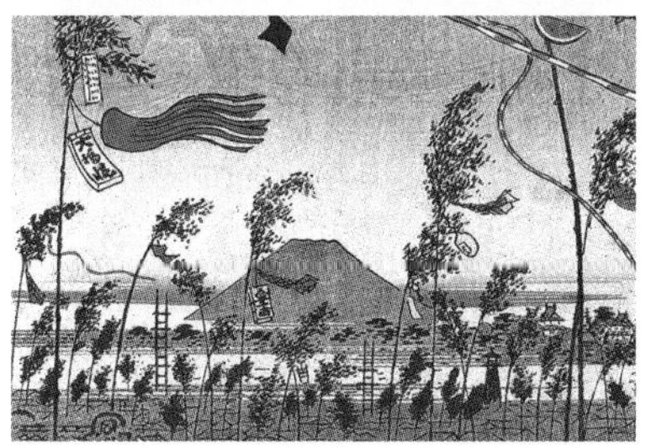

41| Hokusai seizes the moment. Along the winding route between the rice paddies of Ejiri, travelers are suddenly surprised by a violent gust of autumnal wind. Pieces of paper and hats fly around at the wind's whim, to the great chagrin of the travelers, who bend over, hanging on to their clothes. Mount Fuji, indifferent to the scene, is barely visible in the background.

42| For a series about famous places in Kyoto, Sadanobu offered a view of Kōzan-ji ("high mountain temple") and its craggy landscape. The place, so famous for its bright red maple trees, was particularly popular in fall. However, here the artist represents the Buddhist temple in the rain, solitary and lost in a somber, tormented sky.

43| On a gentle night with a full moon, the poetic symbol of fall, a pleasure boat passes under the arch of the Suehiro Bridge. The passengers abord lean over to enjoy the calm and serene landscape. Perched on the *taiko-bashi*, a man thoughtfully observes the enormous moon, whose size the theatrical Gakutei deliberately exaggerated.

44| Around 1790, Tsutaya Jūzaburō published a trilogy of poetic anthologies on the theme of *Setsugekka*. To illustrate the seventy-eight *kyōka* poems of the volume on snow, Utamaro drew five winter landscapes. Here, two fishermen are bringing a boat back to shore. Like lost spirits in the snow, they battle the elements, doubled over in effort, melding into a peaceful, cold nature. A virtuoso, Utamaro plays with the different shades of gray and transparency. A translucent, spectral weeping willow, a symbol of permanence associated with the afterlife, opens the foreground.

41 | Katsushika Hokusai
Ejiri in Suruga Province
Series: *Thirty-six Views of Mount Fuji*,
publisher: Nishimura Yohachi,
ca. 1830–1832
25.1 × 37.5 cm

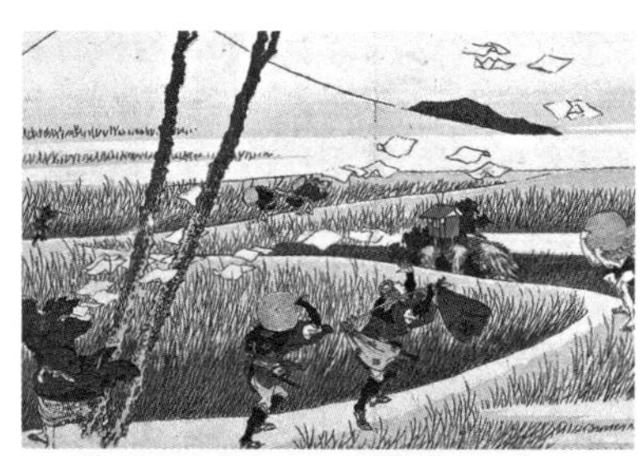

42 | Hasegawa Sadanobu
Rain at Togano
Series: *Famous Places of Kyoto*, publisher:
Wataya Kihei (Wataki), ca. 1870–1871
14.9 × 22.2 cm

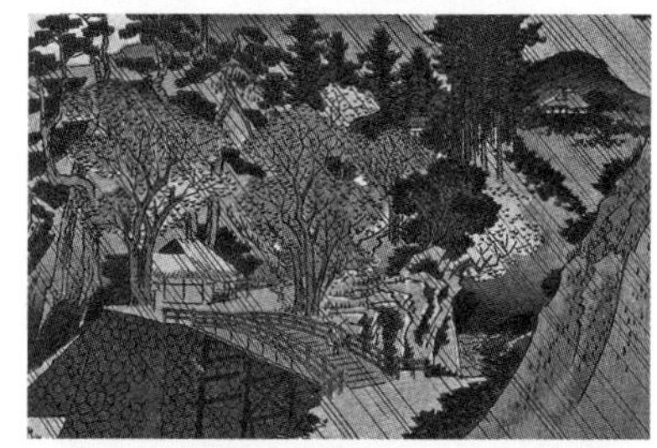

43 | Yashima Gakutei
Moonlight View of Suehiro Bridge
Series: *Famous Places of Naniwa (Osaka),
Glimpses of Tempōzan*, publisher: Shioya
Kisuke (Kōbundō), 1838
25.7 × 37.9 cm

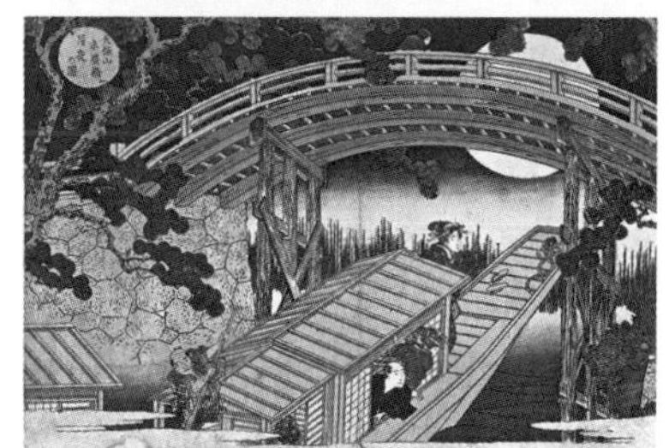

44 | Kitagawa Utamaro
Pulling a Boat in the Snow
Series: *Gin sekai*, publisher: Tsutaya
Jūzaburō (Koshodo), 1790
25.1 × 37.8 cm

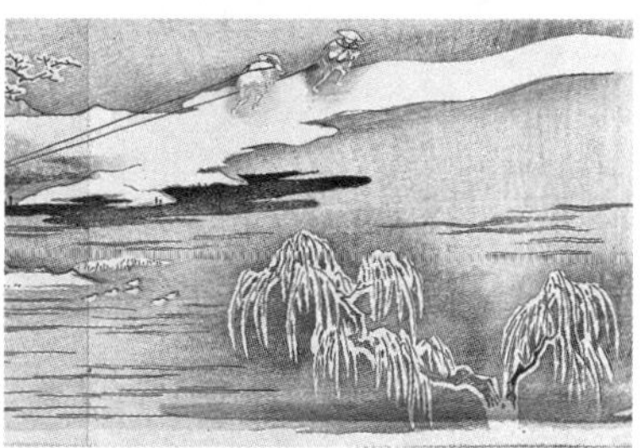

45| For his *Thirty-six Views of Mount Fuji*, Hokusai made several scenes of travelers or pilgrims observing Mount Fuji. Gathered on the terrace of a teahouse overlooking the village of Koishikawa, a group of travelers marvels at the highest peak in Japan. As a maid brings in a platter filled with food, a young woman points to the horizon with an enthusiastic gesture.

46| In the 1830s, for his series on the famous bridges of Japan, Hokusai published a view of the Sano floating bridge, in the province of Kōzuke. Very well-known thanks to the Noh play *Sano no Funabashi* (*The Floating Bridge at Sano*) from the Muromachi period (1336–1573), the bridge (here tossed about by the current), consists of a succession of boats-pontoons connected by thick rigging, with wood planks thrown on top. The brave people who have risked crossing in the snowy weather include a horseman and his guide, who have just left the shore.

47| In his series on the theme of *Setsugekka*, Hokusai symbolizes winter with a snowy landscape in Mukōjima, along the Sumida River. While it was supposed to take place close to the Mokubo Buddhist temple, he represents a tiny shrine—in all likelihood the Umewaka Shrine. It was built in memory of the young Umewakamaru, who was taken away by a slave merchant and died of hunger. His tragic destiny inspired the plot of the Noh play, *Sumidagawa*.

48| Illustrating a poem by Minamoto no Muneyuki (d. 983), a group of five bundled-up hunters warm themselves by a fire one winter evening. The fire's high blazing flames shoot up into the somber mountain sky. On the right, a dilapidated hamlet holds their supplies and the hay mats on which they will sleep.

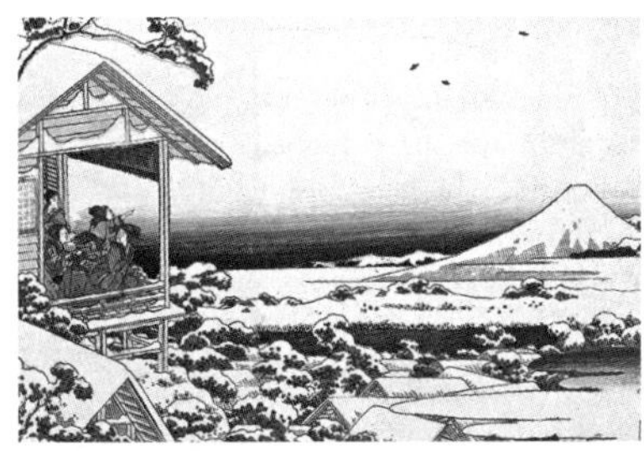

45 | Katsushika Hokusai
Morning after the Snow at Koishikawa in Edo
Series: *Thirty-six Views of Mount Fuji*,
publisher: Nishimura Yohachi (Eijudō),
ca. 1829–1833
25.7 × 38.1 cm

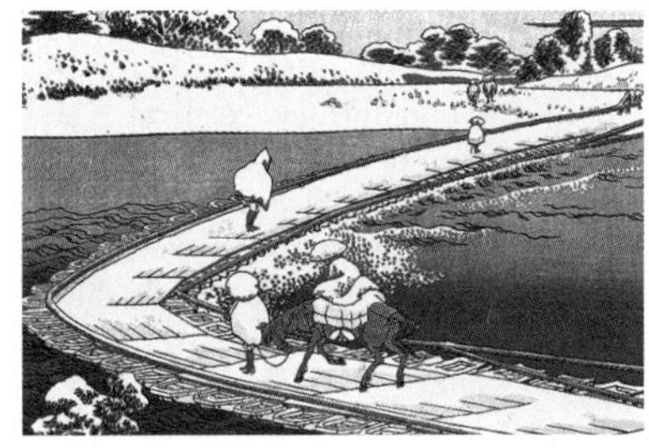

46 | Katsushika Hokusai
Old View of the Boat-bridge at Sano in
Kōzuke Province
Series: *Remarkable Views of Bridges in*
Various Provinces, publisher: Nishimura
Yohachi (Eijudō), ca. 1830
25.7 × 39.4 cm

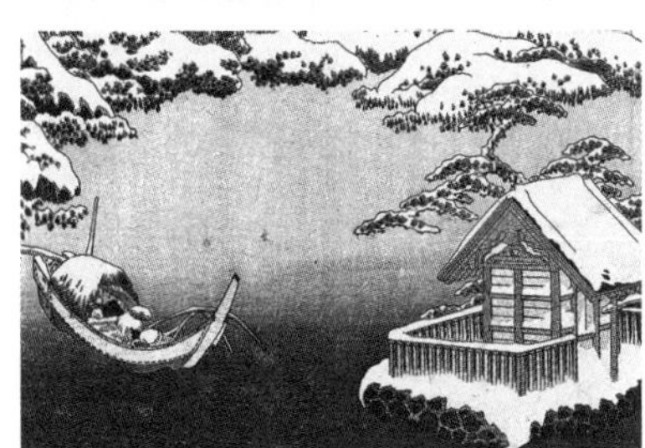

47 | Katsushika Hokusai
Snow on the Sumida River
Series: *Setsugekka*, publisher: Nishimura
Yohachi (Eijudō), 1831–1835
25.5 × 37.1 cm

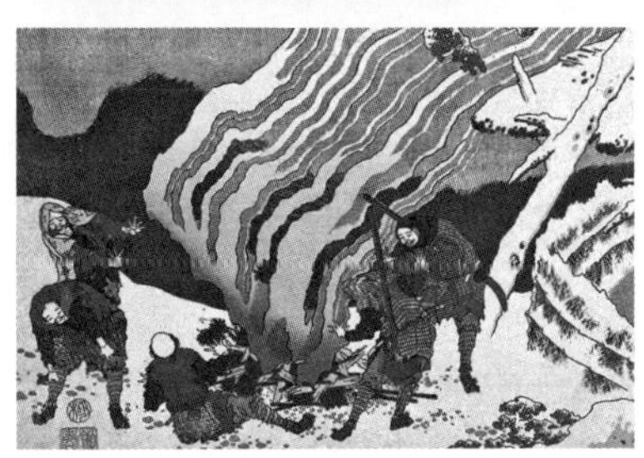

48 | Katsushika Hokusai
Minamoto no Muneyuki
Series: *One Hundred Poems Explained by the*
Nurse, publisher: Iseya Sanjirō (Eijudō),
ca. 1835
25.1 × 36.8 cm

Winter is alone in the mountains' retreat!
Deserted, the earth is bare. When I think of it . . .

49| The Kanbara station, under thick sheets of snow as night falls: the scene is almost phantasmagorical since it rarely snows in this mild region of the Tōkaidō, which is close to the coast and protected by the Kuroshio current. The inventive Hiroshige poetically transposes the station's landscape to winter. On the left a villager, his head protected beneath an umbrella, has his back to the two travelers who, bent over and bundled up in their clothes, climb the mountain as best they can.

50| A daimyo procession climbs the craggy slopes of a snow-covered mountain to reach the fortified castle of Kameyama. The military fortress, now in ruins, was also used as an inn for travelers. As he often did for winter landscapes, Hiroshige limits the colors of the sky and characters, who are dressed in hefty blue coats and coiffed with their ubiquitous yellow straw hats. The only flourish of color is the subtle shading of pink evoking the sunrise. As in the previous view, Hiroshige (who saw this station in summer), transposed the scene to winter.

51| Even though he drew a daimyo procession arriving at the Fujikawa station in high summer for the Hōeidō version of *Fifty-three Stations of the Tōkaidō*, here Hiroshige represents a snow-covered landscape, in this lesser known, small-format edition, published by Sanoya Kihei. A horseman and his guide are at the center, braving the snowstorm as they descend the steep slope leading to the station. In 1855, Hiroshige transposed the composition to a vertical format with *Snow at Yamanaka Village nearby Fujikawa*, for a new version of the Tōkaidō.

52| Hiroshige finished his series *Eight Views in the Environs of Edo*, illustrating a *kyōka* poem by Taihaidō Nomimasu. The pictorial genre of "eight views" (*hakkei*) was explored extensively by Hiroshige and the *ukiyo-e* artists as of the second half of the eighteenth century. Inspired by the Chinese landscapes of the "eight views of Xiaoxiang," along with the derivative "eight views of Ōmi," an amalgamation of the most beautiful views from Lake Biwa, he always ended up with a wintry nighttime scene.

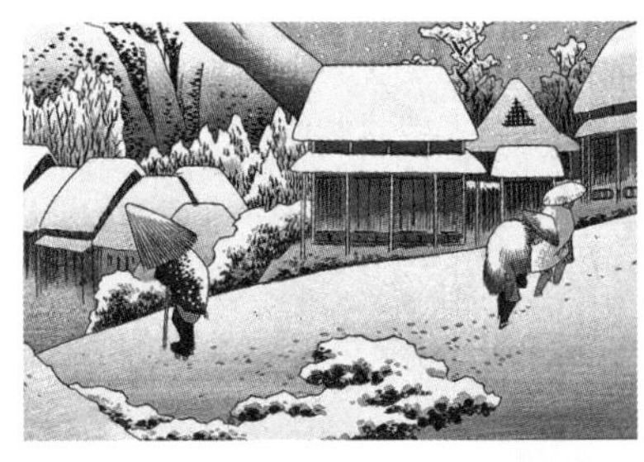

49 | Utagawa Hiroshige
Evening Snow at Kanbara
Series: *Fifty-three Stations of the Tōkaidō*,
publisher: Takenouchi Magohachi
(Hōeidō), ca. 1833–1834
22.5 × 34.9 cm

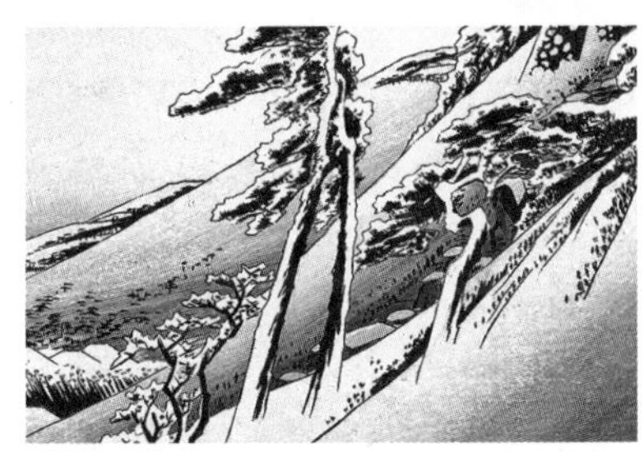

50 | Utagawa Hiroshige
Clear Weather after Snow
Series: *Fifty-three Stations of the Tōkaidō*,
publisher: Takenouchi Magohachi
(Hōeidō), ca. 1833–1834
23.8 × 35.9 cm

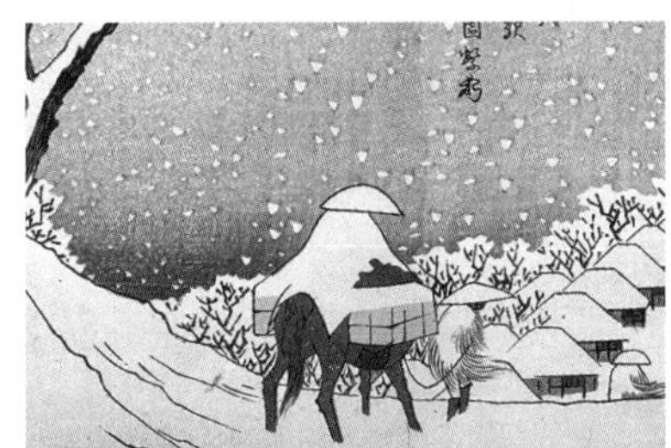

51 | Utagawa Hiroshige
Fujikawa
Series: *Fifty-three Stations of the Tōkaidō*,
publisher: Sanoya Kihei (Kikakudō),
ca. 1838
17 × 23.2 cm

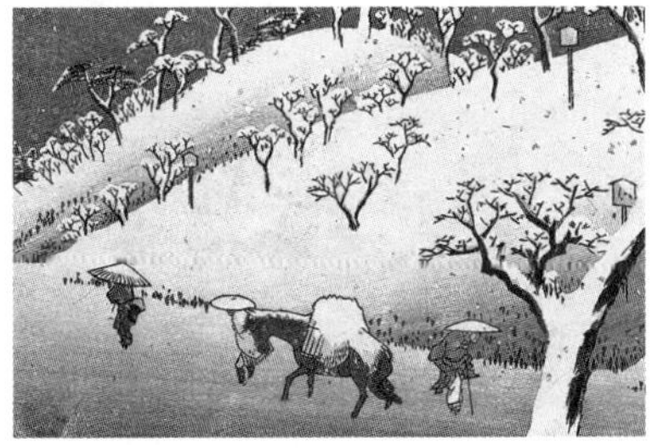

52 | Utagawa Hiroshige
Asukayama in Evening Snow
Series: *Eight Views in the Environs of Edo*,
publisher: Sanoya Kihei (Kikakudō),
ca. 1838
22.2 × 34.9 cm

*The snow covers the signs that forbid
breaking off the cherry tree branches, and breaks
them, too.*
Taihaidō Nomimasu

53| Between 1835 and 1842, Hiroshige created a series on the famous restaurants of Edo for the publisher Fujiokaya Hikotarō. At nightfall, three young women, lifting up their clothing due to the snow, climb onto the pontoon of the Uekya restaurant in the Mokubo Temple, along the Sumida River. In the background, a customer takes a moment to contemplate the night from one of the establishment's balconies.

54| Glancing over the snow-covered plain in Susaki along Edo Bay, a golden eagle gets ready to swoop in on its prey. Humans, always present in Hiroshige's work, are suggested by small houses and by a sawmill that is just barely visible at the left of the composition. A single pail floats in the middle of the marsh, a very tiny residue of the human imprint, entertaining a group of birds. Hiroshige utilizes an original composition, playing with the contrast between the close-up view of the eagle and the snow-covered landscape, which extends toward the horizon all the way to Mount Tsukuba.

55| In the same (amazingly colorful) series as the previous view, Hiroshige represents the very popular entry to Sensōji, the oldest temple in Edo, in the district of Asakusa, which is dedicated to the bodhisattva goddess Kannon. He juxtaposes red with white, creating an original, very lively composition. In the foreground, the Kaminarimon ("door of thunder") and its imposing lantern open the scene to the viewer who, at the same level as the visitor, can thus enjoy a view of the Hōzōmon ("door to the room of treasures") that hides the temple.

56| Itahana-juku was the fourteenth station of the Kiso Kaidō road. Along the river, as the sun sets on the horizon, a group of travelers takes a path edged with pine trees to reach the entry to the village. The entire piece is accented with bold colors, notably on the clothing of the characters, in contrast with the white of the snow. Eisen inventively depicts the flow of water by coloring the riverbank green.

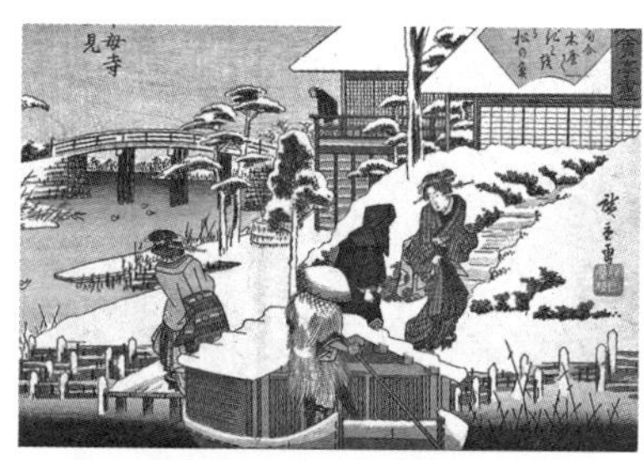

53 | Utagawa Hiroshige
Uekya Restaurant at Mokuboji
Series: *Famous Restaurants of Edo*,
publisher: Fujiokaya Hikotarō
(Shōgendō), ca. 1835–1842
23.8 × 36 cm

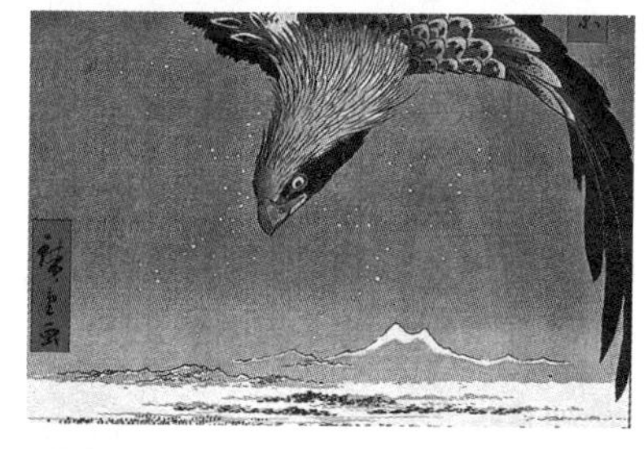

54 | Utagawa Hiroshige
Jūmantsubo Plain at Fukagawa Susaki
Series: *One Hundred Famous Views of Edo*,
publisher: Uoya Eikichi (or Sakanaya
Eikichi), May 1857
35.7 × 24.1 cm

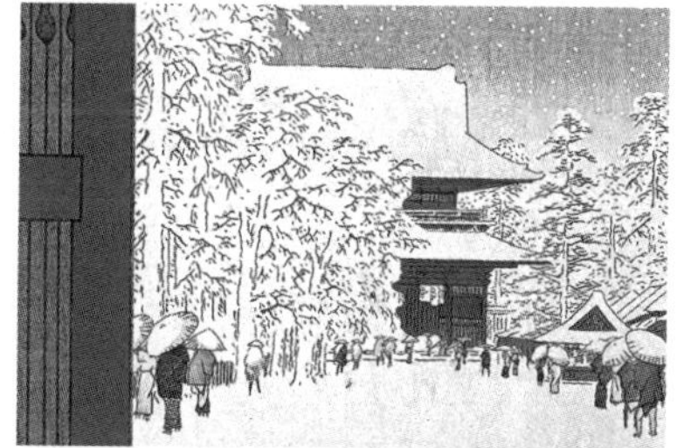

55 | Utagawa Hiroshige
Kinryūsan Temple at Asakusa
Series: *One Hundred Famous Views of Edo*,
publisher: Uoya Eikichi (or Sakanaya
Eikichi), July 1856
35.7 × 24.1 cm

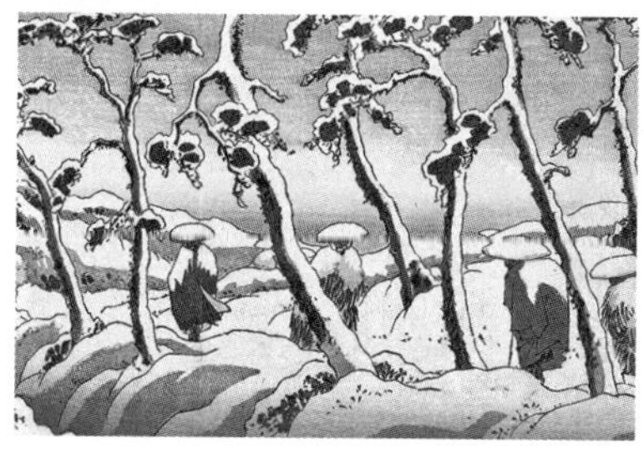

56 | Keisai Eisen
Itahana
Series: *Sixty-nine Stations of the Kiso Kaidō*,
publisher: Iseya Rihei (Kinjudō),
ca. 1835–1842
21.9 × 34.3 cm

57| The solitary Nichiren (1222–1282) laboriously climbs the steep slope of a mountain, his bare calves covered in snow. A great admirer of the legendary historical characters of his country, Kuniyoshi represents the Buddhist monk, who was exiled on Sado Island between 1271 and 1274 after being abandoned by his enemies at a dilapidated shrine nearby the Tsukahara cemetery. His back turned, dressed in red, he struggles, alone but determined, against a snowstorm. Here, Kuniyoshi uses Nichiren (whose fraught life inspired countless legends) as an allegory for triumphant faith.

58| Hasui depicts, in shades of white and blue, a lakeside landscape covered in snow. At the center, alongside a tiny skiff, a boatman transports his passenger to the shore of Ushibori, on the opposite bank of the river. In the background, village homes are reflected in the calm, peaceful water of the lake. A few glowing windows provide subtle warmth to this composition, with its cold, solitary setting.

59| Partially turned away, bundled up in traditional dress, a woman, her face concealed underneath her umbrella, climbs the stairs of the Zōjō-ji, a famous Buddhist temple in Chiba Park in Tokyo, and *bodaiji* ("bodhi temple," meaning a funeral temple) of the Tokugawa clan. Covered in snow, the building stands out against a somber gray sky. In the foreground, a pine tree blocks the lower left corner, following a type of composition that Hokusai and Hiroshige had already used extensively.

60| Facing away, protecting himself from the storm with a large umbrella, a man dressed in black, modern clothing, heads toward the Zōjō-ji, the preferred subject of Hasui, a master of ambiance, who delivers a deeply melancholic work of art here. The Tokugawa clan's *bodaiji*, emerging from a somber sky as a great symbol of the past and the Edo period, here confronts the modern world and the tireless progress of humans.

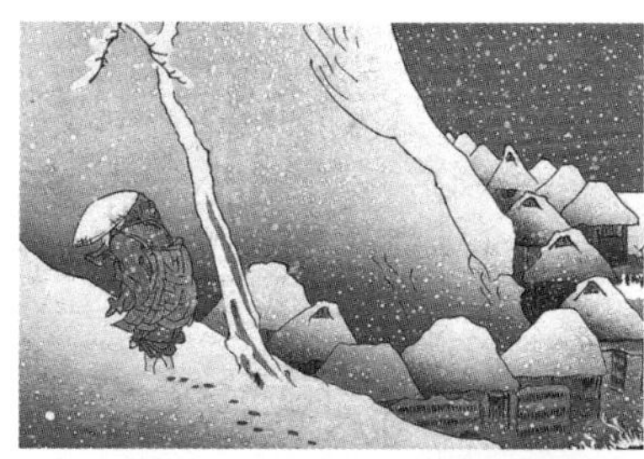

57 | Utagawa Kuniyoshi
Nichiren in Snow at Tsukahara, Sodo Province
Series: *Sketches of the Life of the Great Priest*, publisher: Iseya Rihei (Kinjudō), ca. 1835–1837
25.5 × 37 cm

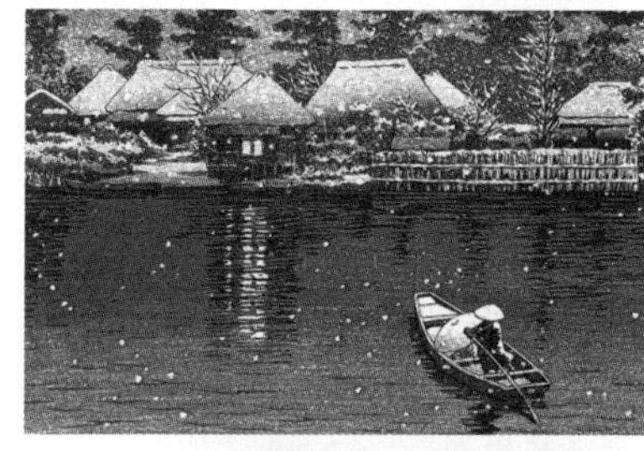

58 | Kawase Hasui
Ushibori
Publisher: Shōzaburō Watanabe, 1930
26 × 38.9 cm

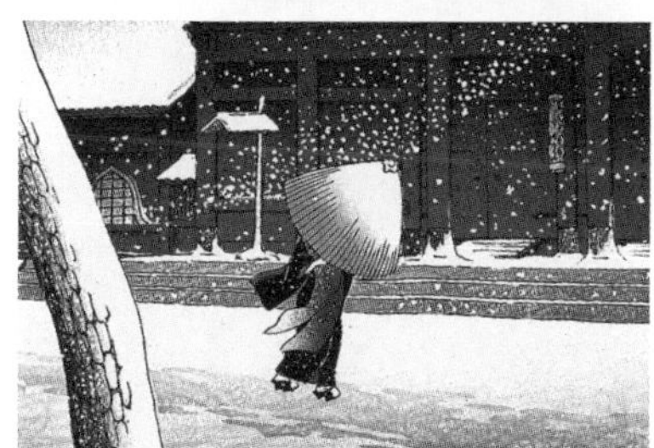

59 | Kawase Hasui
The Temple Zōjō-ji in Shiba
Series: *Twenty Views of Tokyo*, publisher: Shōzaburō Watanabe, 1925
38.7 × 26.3 cm

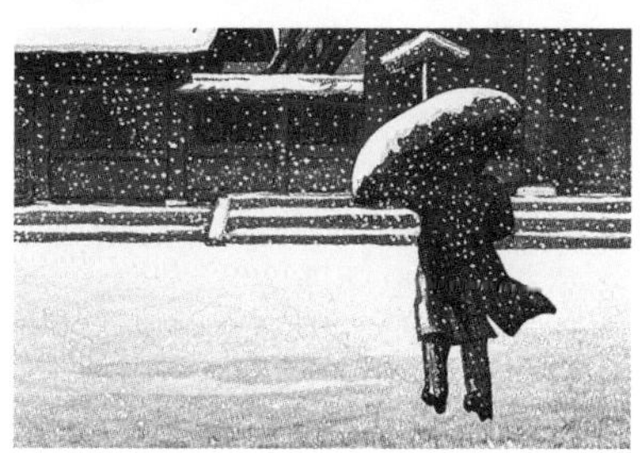

60 | Kawase Hasui
Snow at Zōjō-ji Temple
Series: *Souvenirs of Travel, Second Series*, publisher: Shōzaburō Watanabe, January 1922
39.7 × 25.8 cm

Photo Credits

Freer and Sackler Galleries, Washington, DC: 60
Museum of Fine Arts, Boston: 39
Rijksmuseum, Amsterdam: 8, 9, 11, 14, 29, 31, 37, 44, 47, 57, 58, 59
The Metropolitan Museum of Art, New York: 1, 2, 3, 4, 5, 6, 7, 10, 12, 13, 15, 16, 17, 18, 19, 20, 21, 22, 23, 24, 25, 26, 27, 28, 30, 32, 33, 34, 35, 36, 38, 40, 41, 42, 43, 45, 46, 48, 49, 50, 51, 52, 53, 54, 55, 56

Acknowledgments

I would like to thank the whole team at Éditions Hazan, Anne-Isabelle Vannier, Jérôme Gille, and Marie-Hélène Durand de Corbiac for their trust and enthusiasm, my colleague and friend Pierre Hamard for his kindness and advice, Renaud Bezombes for his attentive proofreading, as well as Laurence Mignon, Maryse Manach, Frédéric Wronski, Julie Richaud, and Charlène Boulay.